Give me eyes to see

Lorella Rouster

How God used a painful autistic childhood to give me eyes to see and help the hurting, forgotten children of Africa

Every Child Ministries

2022

Copyright © 2022 by Every Child Ministries

All rights reserved. This book or any portion thereof may not be reproduced or used in any manner whatsoever without the express written permission of the publisher except for the use of brief quotations in a book review or scholarly journal.

First Printing: 2022

ISBN 978-1-387-56510-8

Every Child Ministries
PO Box 810
Hebron, IN, 466341

www.ecmafrica.org
www.mwindaproject-ecm.com
www.teachingforafrica.com

Ordering Information:
Special discounts are available on quantity purchases by corporations, associations, educators, and others. For details, contact the publisher at the above listed address.

U.S. trade bookstores and wholesalers: Please contact Every Child Ministries, Lorella Rouster, Tel: 219-299-1919 Fax: 219-996-4203, Attention: Lorella, or email lrouster@ecmafrica.org .

Dedication

To my honey, my best friend, my partner who puts up with piles of huge archive notebooks in the living room and always encourages me. Without you, none of this could have happened. I dedicate this book to you, my beloved husband John.

Table of Contents: Page

1. Seeing the children chased away from church—Zaire, now Congo, The Sunday School Project (1981)..15

2. Seeing children in the schools of Ghana, Character Building from the Bible (1999)..83

3. Seeing Street Children—Ghana (1999)........93

4. Seeing Homeless Children-- Haven of Hope, Ghana (2001)....................99

5. Seeing Slave Children--Initiative vs. Shrine Slavery, Ghana (1999)..........................127

6. Seeing Trafficked Children, Ghana & Uganda (2009)...155

7. Seeing War-Affected children, N Uganda (2006)...161

8. Seeing Children Rejected because of Albinism, N Uganda (2007)..175

9. Seeing Children living under persecution, South Sudan, (2006)...181

10. Seeing Beggar Children--Karimojong & The Karamoja Homeland, Uganda................ 185

11. Seeing Children Taught by Teachers with no Lessons and no Bibles--The Mwinda Project, Congo,(2015)...191

12. Seeing the Deaf (Congo, 2022)............... 201
Timeline...211
Endnotes..217
Short-Term Missionaries & Others Who Shared Our Journey (1983-2015)............................222

Forward:

Why I always notice those others have forgotten

As I mentioned in my first book, God Uses CROOKED STICKS, I believe my attraction for the downtrodden stems from my own painful childhood. I was not abused. My pain stemmed from my innate shyness and my feelings of inadequacy and fears that I would not be accepted.

How and why my personality developed as it did, well, that's another subject, but the fact is that these feelings paralyzed me socially throughout my entire childhood and well into my teen years. In fact, I was so paralyzed socially that I do not remember speaking to any of my peers throughout elementary and junior high school. Ever. Not a single "hi" through all those years, much less a conversation.

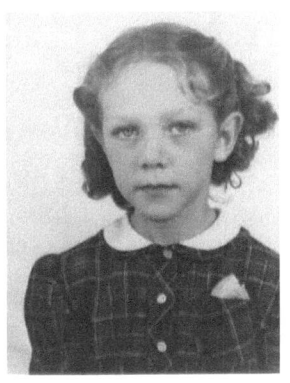

My Kindergarten picture. Doesn't my shyness just exude from it?

No, there was one exception to that. I think I was in seventh grade. I was feeling so isolated and lonely sitting by myself to eat my lunch every day, then just walking aimlessly around town until the noon hour ended. A more confident girl would have just plunked herself down with a group of kids and said, "Hi." That was terrifying to me. So I planned and practiced for months and months. Finally I got up my courage enough to go up to one of the girls that normally sat in a group. Somehow I asked if it would be OK if I sat with them to eat my lunch. She said she'd talk it over with the group and let me know. The next day she came to me and said, "We talked about it, and we decided we already have enough kids sitting with us." So, my deepest fears were true. No one wanted me. That is how I interpreted it. After that I felt more embarrassed than ever to sit alone, because I had been officially rejected.

Though I never felt the need to seek an official diagnosis, I am totally convinced that if I was growing up today instead of in the 1940's and 50's, I would have been considered as somewhere on the autism spectrum. I had never heard of such a thing back then, and I doubt that my parents had, either. I just knew that although I longed to interact with others at times, I had absolutely no idea how to do such a thing. On a scale of 0 to 100, my social score was minus 50. How could I have a social score when I didn't talk to anybody? During my elementary school days, I mostly lived in a fantasy world of my own making. When I entered that fantasy world, I would often wring my hands and breathe heavily, actions I now recognize as 'stimming,' common among us on the autism spectrum.

As I came into junior high, I became desperately and painfully aware of my aloneness. I felt rejected, though looking back, I realize I was totally unfriendly. I did not dislike people. I longed to be 'popular' and daydreamed about it all the time. Interacting with people just felt unnatural and uncomfortable to me. It filled me with fear like nothing else.

About the same time that the group of girls rejected my offer to sit with them at lunchtime, I began to think about trying to interact with a guy who had a locker next to me. I did not have a crush on him or any special attraction to him. I just wanted to speak to somebody, and being nearby, he seemed like a good candidate. In my fantasy world, I began practicing how to speak to him. "Hey, how ya' doing'? I'm Lorella." No, that wasn't me. I'd never be able to pull that off.

"Excuse me, please. I don't believe I've had the honor of meeting you." No, too formal.

"Hi." Maybe, but the year went by and I never did find the nerve even to say hi, though I practiced it in my mind thousands of times.

When I gave my life to Jesus Christ and was born again at age 15, those feelings of insecurity slowly began to subside, thank God. I knew that the God of the Universe loved me, and I began to focus not on how others perceived me, but learning more about Him and pleasing Him.

That made an immediate and huge difference, but it still took me many years to learn to approach others. I had only a couple of dates, which confirmed in my young mind that there must be something wrong with me. On the dates I did have, I don't remember talking at all. I was content (thrilled) just to be with a guy and to be seen with a guy. It meant I was OK, but the comfort was short-lived. The guys never asked me out again.

I didn't understand then that I was probably the most boring date in the world, and that guys probably felt I was uninterested in them because I'm sure I didn't ask them even one question about themselves, or even talk hardly at all.

I well remember the deep pain and constant loneliness of my earlier years. How many dances did I go to and sit all alone, watching others laughing and enjoying themselves? Wishing that somebody would ask me to dance? Then walking home alone without having danced at all and without having spoken to a single person.

I was in fact an outcast, though I realize it was of my own making. I know what it is like to be alone, to feel unwanted, unaccepted, unloved by my peers. It is an unending pain in the soul. So after I became a Christian, I was always aware of the shy person in the corner, the one sitting alone, the one not entering into activities, the one bullied or ridiculed. I readily recognized people who seemed almost invisible to others. I was drawn to them because I had been one of them.

When I went to Africa as a missionary in mid-life, I found myself naturally identifying with groups of children who were outcaste for any reason. I felt such an empathy for them, such an identification with them, that usually I immediately began praying for them and trying to plan ways to reach out to them.

This book is the true story of how God led me twelve times to start projects to reach African children for Christ, emphasizing what Jesus called "the least of these" (Matthew 25:40). It's been quite a ride, and it hasn't ended yet. Come along, and let's backtrack together.

1. Seeing children chased away from church —The Sunday School Project, Zaire, now Congo (1981)

The Motivation for the Sunday School Project

When our family went to Congo (then Zaire) on June 22, 1981[i], we saw a heart-rending situation in many villages. Few people in the village had a watch, and there were no church bells to call people to worship, but there were often old tire rims or other metal objects hung from a tree branch. The church leaders would bang on it with a metal rod or whatever they could find to call people to worship.

The children were always the first to come. They came immediately when they heard the sound of the gong. Often, they filled the church, singing enthusiastically. However, they never got any Bible teaching, and never were permitted to participate in the worship service. There were too many of them. They took up all the seats so that there was no room for the adults. Church deacons announced that it was time for the children to leave, but they did not want to go. When they did not cooperate, the deacons often resorted to chasing them out with sticks.

Then they usually went outside and crowded around all the window, looking in to see what was going on in the service. This was permitted up to a point, but their bodies often blocked air movement. With perspiring people inside, the children at the windows frequently cut off air flow, causing the people inside to become hotter and more uncomfortable. As this happened, the deacons usually chased the children away with sticks.

We were shocked to see this, but we did understand why it was done. We did not enjoy being in a church building with the windows blocked by human bodies, either.

Yet we innately knew that something was very wrong with this scenario. Wasn't it Jesus Himself who said, *"Let the little children come to Me, and do not forbid them..."?* (Luke 18:16 NKJV)

When I asked why they did not teach the children at some other time, the leaders responded that no one knew how to do that. Immediately I began to think about the training and experience God had allowed my husband John and I to have. Maybe we could be part of the solution to this problem.

Even right at the mission station Nkara where our family was serving, I saw that although there was a fairly large church body, and a large cement church building, nothing was currently being done to reach the children. Missionaries had previously had a Sunday school there in the old days, but our co-workers the Smiths' energies were being consumed with the establishment of the Bible school for pastors' training—Ecole Biblique Laban, village evangelism, and the home-schooling of their own children.

Starting the first Sunday school

I hardly knew enough of the language to put a whole sentence together yet,[ii] but I was determined to start a Sunday school at Nkara. It would not be held at the same time as the worship service, but at another hour so that the children could also receive Bible teaching.

That first week, after developing the lesson in English, I spent at least fifteen hours painstakingly translating it into Kikongo. Of course, writing anything from the Bible greatly stretched my developing vocabulary.

In addition, I was still at the stage of thinking first in English and then searching for the right Kituba words. But this resulted in sentences constructed in English, even if the words were in Kituba. I hadn't yet learned how sentences are constructed in Kituba, but still I put forth my best effort. Finally, the lesson was ready. I was still at the point that pretty much all I could do was to read it, using as much expression as I could.

Word went out that there was going to be a Sunday school for children at Nkara Ewa. The Sunday it was to open, I had eaten breakfast, and was still relaxing in my robe and slippers enjoying a cup of coffee, when Nicol Smith[iii], the daughter of our missionary neighbors, came running over to our house. "Aunt Lorella!" she called. "The church is already full of kids waiting for Sunday school to start." I stepped outside our home and looked down the hill at the church building.

Nicol was right. There were lots of kids inside, and more were coming down the paths from several directions.[iv] I knew I could not leave the children alone in the church, so I quickly got dressed, grabbed my Kituba New Testament and my teaching materials, and walked down the sandy path to the church.

The children all listened attentively, but at the conclusion of the lesson, I asked some girls if they understood. Hesitating, they answered, "Yes, a little." I bet it was very little indeed! Yet, it was a beginning. I kept working on the language and I kept developing lessons. Gradually, my Kituba improved.

First Sunday School at Nkara Ewa. Our children and the Smiths are on the left—Sharon, Shawn and Nicol Smith, in the middle, John Henry and Todd Smith, on the right, Carrie.

It was our practice always to give an invitation to those who may not yet have a personal relationship with Christ. After experimenting with several ways of doing this, we settled on designating a place where seekers might come after class to find help in trusting Christ and assurance of salvation. Many, many children made professions of faith during those days.

Often adults also sat in on the Sunday schools, or listened in on the side. One day, our family was enjoying a meal together when someone knocked at the door. Our cook Mapiya opened the door and found it was the chief of one of the local villages. "The chief of Nsiengobo is at the door," he informed us. It was worth interrupting our meal when he informed us that he, too, had received Christ as his Savior through the teaching he had heard "on the side" in Sunday school.

The children loved skits as a part of the Bible lessons. They loved to participate in them, and they loved to watch them. They had no inhibitions. If pigs were in the story, they were glad to become pigs, crawling around on the (usually) dirt floors, even squealing like pigs.

The Congolese would go to elaborate lengths to develop the skits, too, especially for holidays. I remember a skit for a Christmas lesson where

Herod's soldiers came marching in wearing sunglasses made of a very soft balsam-like local wood called mikobodi, and bearing carved wooden guns on their shoulders. A star was pulled on a string across the church, and Mary carried a live baby "Jesus."

Developing the Sunday schools involved a constant process of learning. Since we knew how much the Congolese[v] liked skits, we decided to prepare a more realistic-looking skit to teach the account of Jesus healing a leper. We prepared one of the Bible school students with ragged clothing and gave him cold cream to put on his arms, legs, and face to resemble leprous sores. He came in the side door unannounced, crying out, "Mvindu! Mvindu!" (Unclean! Unclean!)

Pow! The moment the children heard the word 'unclean', they all jumped up together and ran out the other door just as fast as their legs could take them.

I ran down the road after them, shouting, "Come back! It's not real. It's just a skit." Four or five children were finally coaxed back, out of about 80 who had been there before. However, most of the children came back the following week and continued to come to Sunday school. We learned our lesson, and from that time on we always announced that a skit was about to take place.

Another Sunday school skit I remember I observed many years later. One of women teachers we had trained made herself the donkey and allowed a child to "ride" her into "Jerusalem," while others picked and waved flowers with joy.

Keeping the children's attention in Sunday school was rarely a problem. Usually they were attentive and eager to take in every word. That's why I was surprised one day when I was teaching Sunday school, when all-of-a-sudden, every single student jumped up and ran outside. What was going on?

I went to the window and saw the children jumping into the air, grabbing something, and putting their hands to their mouths, again and again. Then I realized what was happening. The termites were "swarming," coming up out of the ground. Termites were considered a special delicacy, so the children were taking advantage of the situation to indulge in a special, on-the-spot treat. I wasn't sure whether we were finished with Sunday school for the day, but after the swarming finished, about 15-20 minutes, the children came back, sat down and looked up at me as if nothing had happened. I opened my Bible again, and we finished the lesson.

The Congolese love to sing, and sing as they work and live every day, with great gusto. I learned many of their songs, and some of the hymns that had been translated by missionaries before me, and collected in a little song book called "Kintwadi" (fellowship). However, often I wished we had other songs in Kituba. After a time, I tried translating songs and even writing some. This required a vocabulary and understanding of the language that enabled me to consider several different ways to say the same thing. One of my favorite songs that I translated was "This Is the Day that the Lord Has Made." It caught on quickly and is still being sung throughout the Kituba-speaking region of Congo.

One of the most important songs that I wrote is "Mbotika ta Gulusa Nge Ve," (Baptism Will Not Save You). I wrote this because strong Catholic influence had led even many Protestants to believe that they were born again in the waters of baptism.

I knew that this teaching was not only unbiblical, but very dangerous. If one believes he is already saved because he was baptized as a baby, what further need is there to come to Christ for salvation? I saw over and over how the false teaching of baptismal regeneration gave people a false sense of security. I talked to many who had never repented of their sins and trusted Christ for salvation, yet they believed they were children of God because they were baptized as infants. It was hard for such people to see their need of trusting Christ as Savior. I knew I needed to do something to counteract this teaching that was keeping people in darkness while assuring them they were in the light. The song was sung widely all over the Nkara area, so at least people were forced to think about their relationship to Christ.

The song that came to be most identified with Sunday school was "Kiese Mingi"—I'm so happy. It was used as a song to announce Sunday school and call children to come. It also was used whenever the children began to get a little too rowdy, to regain their attention. The teacher just began singing "Kiese Mingi," and the children would immediately stop their ruckus and join in the song. Afterwards, the teacher could begin teaching again, and the children would listen.

Training others to reach children

About the time we were starting the first Sunday school, our missionary colleague Jim Smith, who was in charge of the Bible school, 'Ecole Biblique Laban,' asked me to teach a class on Christian Education. That involved more preparing of lessons, now both for the children's Sunday school and also for the Bible school students. This again kept stretching my ability in Kituba. When I made a language mistake in my Bible school classes, the students would correct me, and this helped a lot. In January, I began sending the students out to open new Sunday schools in neighboring villages[vi]. Every week, in addition to Christian education class, I also taught a teacher training class in which I demonstrated the Sunday school lesson for the coming week.

Some of the Sunday schools were taught in larger church buildings constructed of cement blocks. Others were in village churches where the tiny mud-and-stick structure might hold 20 people. The Sunday schools drew many more children than that. In some cases the children stood throughout the entire teaching. At times they were so closely packed there was literally no room to move. In one memorable incident, a boy of about ten years reached his arm up to scratch his nose. Meanwhile, others pressed in, so that when he tried to put it

The thatch shelter where I am teaching is where the local village church meets.

back down just a moment later, there was no room left for him to lower it.

In other cases, we held the Sunday school outside in front of the church. We wanted to be as close to the church meeting place as possible so as to identify the Sunday school with it in the children's minds. In one village called Mathu, the thatch roof hung down quite low, so when I taught there, I propped my Bible and extra teaching materials on the church roof when not in use.

Me teaching with one of the Bible school students at the village of Mathu. Notice my Bible on the roof.

Some of the Sunday schools had benches for the children to sit on. In other places, they stood through the teaching or sat on woven grass mats. The only materials were those we were providing, all made by hand. One summer we held a Vacation Bible School at Nkara. Our daughters Carrie and Sharon helped with teaching. For that special occasion, we provided crayons and paper for drawing. When Carrie distributed the crayons, the children just sat there staring at them. What were they supposed to do with these? It took quite a bit of demonstration before the children understood that they could draw and color with them—something they had never dreamed of doing.

By the end of our time at Nkara, there were sixteen active Sunday schools all around us. In addition, the students at Bible school Laban had been introduced to the importance of teaching children, had some instruction in how to do so, and had beginning experience in teaching children in Sunday school.

During those years, my work was made lighter by Cindy Hawkins, who stayed with us for nine months, teaching our son John Henry. My husband John was kept busy with construction projects, procuring supplies, overseeing a medical clinic, and developing a garden to enhance the diet of the Bible school students. Carrie and Sharon also taught a women's literacy class, so all the family kept busy.

During their Christmas vacations, we had sent the Bible school students out equipped with Bible lessons and the assignment to gather and teach the children in their own home villages and those around them. The students took this assignment very seriously, and returned with reports of hundreds of children professing faith in Christ for the first time.

At the end of that time, I also had put into Kituba the basic principles I myself had learned through Child Evangelism Fellowship and years of experience in teaching at home.

During the years 1984-1989, we were in the States. Our marriage needed some major strengthening at that time, and my husband John wanted our children to finish high school here. John got a job in Northwest Indiana with Associated Milk Producers as a field representative in charge of quality control. The pay was quite modest, so we used funds from the sale of our farm to supplement our personal living.

John allowed me to work full time to develop a new mission organization we founded called "Every Child Ministries." ECM received its Certificate of Incorporation on December 4, 1985. On April 24 of the following year, the new mission received tax-exempt status from the IRS. In 1986, ECM published its first annual report, showing 26 new Sunday schools and the publication of our first 200 Sunday school training manuals in Kituba. Our total budget was $ 8,373.[vii]

I spent most of my time further developing the training program I had started at Nkara. During that time, I wrote the above-mentioned teacher training manual that was eventually translated into six languages spoken in Africa.[viii] I also talked through the training in Kituba as if I were presenting it in person, and recorded it in our living room on cassette tapes using a Sony "boombox."

Each summer, I traveled to Africa, usually with small teams of helpers,[ix] and trained teachers all over the Bandundu Province, wherever the church sent me. In those years, neither ECM nor our family had our own dedicated vehicle, so the team and I traveled as most Congolese do. We hitchhiked rides on commercial trucks that were transporting manioc and other crops to town and taking goods from the city into the interior. At the end of the training, the church that had welcomed the team received a set of the cassette tapes and a hand-wind tape player to enable them to review the training.

I had many adventures in those years. The training in Bulungu was most memorable. I had traveled by canoe on a river and was quite tired when we reached the town. There were no steps up the steep river bank, so I had to scale it with the help of a stick and occasionally a strong hand from one of the pastors. Then we had to walk to the church. Once we got up the bank, the ground was level, but the sun was beating down in full force. We walked what seemed like a very long distance. I became so tired that I just closed my eyes and kept putting one foot in front of another, staying between the pastors whom I could hear talking on each side of me.

When we finally arrived, the church service was just getting over. We were not able to greet the people, but they had received the message that we were on our way, confirming that the training seminar would take place the following day. I didn't see any chairs, so I lay down on the ground in the shade of a tree and poured water from my drinking bottle over my face and arms.

Finally, I was taken to my room—a simple room with a bed, a small table and a cement floor. I lay down and slept all afternoon. About supper time the pastors called me, saying I needed to get up. "Why should I get up?" I responded, and continued lying there, still exhausted. I never did get up until the following morning.

That night, the bed I was lying on broke down. Congolese beds are made with a platform that fits into a framework, but often it fits too loosely, so that when any weight is placed on the bed, it gives way. Still too tired to do anything else, I just continued lying there on the mattress, lying tilted half on the floor. The next day the pastors fixed my bed for me.

When I settled into my room, I set my suitcase of teaching materials I had brought for the churches on the cement floor in my room. I did not realize I set it near a crack in the cement. In the morning, I found that termites had invaded it and turned everything into fine confetti. I took the suitcase outside and soon learned how much chickens love termites, for they came running quickly, sensing a feast.

That same week, I broke through the termite-eaten logs of the outhouse I was using, and fell through the floor up to my shoulders. It was the middle of the night, and no one heard or responded to my cries for help. Fortunately, I was able to grab other logs and placing my feet along the sides of the pit, I eventually wormed my way out. I was scraped and bruised and dirty, but thank God, no serious problems resulted.

Despite all those challenges, I enjoyed a wonderful week of training and many Sunday schools resulted. Many years later, we were able to send Pastor Ipala there to continue and strengthen the work.

During those years, both of our biological daughters, Carrie and Sharon[x], were able to accompany me on the training trips—

Our daughter Sharon gets a big welcome at the church at Dibaya

Sharon in 1987 and Carrie in 1988. In 1987 our good friend Jack Krajnak also went with us. That year we were training at a beautiful place called Lac Hebron, amongst other places, when the local people brought an animal to us tied up in a basket. When they started to untie the basket, I was startled and jumped back. At first it looked like a snake, but it turned out to be an armadillo. We were responsible for providing meals for the trainees who had traveled from their villages and were staying with us for the week, so we bought it for their supper. I remember Jack saying, "Oh, those lucky Congolese!" If I remember right, I think we ate peanut butter sandwiches with local honey.

Sharon, Jack and I add a stone to the foundation of the new church building.

Jack lightened the trip with his sense of humor. I remember one time he looked out at one of the local huts. "I wonder what kind of hut that is," he said. "I don't know, just a hut," Sharon answered. "Hey, isn't that a sign over there by it?" Jack asked.

"Why don't you go over and check it out?" So Sharon went over and turned over the sign Jack had prepared for the joke.

"Well what do you know?" he asked. "It's a Pizza Hut!"

When Carrie helped me, she gave the woman flannelgraph lessons on nutrition which were very well received, and helped with the shopping. She also used her artistic bent to help create more visuals. We were still doing them all by hand at that point.

During most of those years, ECM did not have a computer. We typed our newsletters and our literature on an electric typewriter and added the headlines by painstakingly lining up rub-on letters piece by piece. Pictures were real photographs with a sheet of white dots laid on them to make them come out better when we scanned them. Our first printer took 25 sheets of paper at a time. When the ink cartridge got low, we took it out and shook it and did a few more copies.

We had started ECM in the basement of our home in Cedar Lake, IN with the help of Christian friends. Once or twice a week, a group of friends gathered there to help me make visuals. Hildred Bertsch began serving as volunteer secretary. Everyone who worked with us was a volunteer.

Early in 1988, ECM moved to a small building in Hebron, IN. Though it was a tiny place, it was a big step for us at the time. It was our first time to have a dedicated work space, to pay for heat and electricity. ECM used the small building next to the bigger place we now occupy rent free for several years through the generosity of Helen Bollen.

During those years, God laid on my heart the vision to eventually see a strong, Bible-teaching Sunday school in every village of what was then the Bandundu Province.[xi] That was about 71,000 villages, and six million people at the time, according to a brochure I read.

Our plan was to return to Congo in 1990, after our son John Henry graduated from high school. Our adopted African daughter Kristi[xii] would go with us, continuing her education with home schooling.

On my trip to train teachers at Lac Hebron in 1987, I had asked if there were any other lakes nearby. I knew that swimming every afternoon was a huge benefit to our family when we lived at Nkara. A lake nearby helps so much to help us endure the heat, and getting un-stick-i-fied every day, as we called bathing in the lake, helped reduce the mosquitoes' attraction to us.

The pastors took me through a forest and then a swampy area. On the other side, we came out to a lovely, long, narrow lake which I later learned was called Nkwasanga. (See my book, <u>God Uses CROOKED STICKS</u> for the story of the naming of that place.) I thought it would make a good location for the new training center we planned to build.

The Congolese were quick to congregate in the cities, so we wanted a rural location to encourage at least some of those trained to stay in the interior and serve the neglected rural areas. The location was near several relatively neglected people groups, and I knew that access to water would be a huge boon to our family. I already knew that mosquitoes really zone in on me when I am sweaty.

The lake at Mission Garizim

When I first saw the lake from a hilltop, I remarked, "Oh, it looks dirty and scummy." My guides assured me it was a beautiful, clean, spring-fed lake. They were right. When we got closer, I could see that what I thought was scum was in reality a garden of lily pads with delicate light lavender flowers.

We knew that the new training center would likely attract people from different regions of Congo, speaking different languages, so during my years at home, I had taken classes in French at a local university campus. Congo is a land of 365 languages according to one map I saw, but the colonial language French is the one that unifies the many language groups. It is the language of education, and I knew I needed to learn it in order to train workers from the different provinces.[xiii]

In 1989, I spent six weeks in Quebec in an intensive French program, constantly wearing a button that said, "Je parle français" (I speak French), so that all who saw me would speak to me in French. Theoretically, I could be dismissed from the program if I was caught speaking any language other than French anywhere at any time. (In reality I did not know of anyone who received that penalty. It was mainly just to encourage us to try to speak French all the time.) There were many activities, all carried out in French. I also visited many of the churches of Quebec, Their services, of course, were also in French. There I found one of two scenarios— either a huge cathedral with a congregation of only two or three, or a warm-hearted group of about thirty worshippers—virtually all of them African students also studying at Université Laval.

Part of the expedition leading us through the forest to the second lake.

That same year, John, Kristi and I traveled to Congo to see the property for the training center. It had been promised to us by the local church there.

They had arranged for all the local chiefs to gather and give us the land on the western bank of the lake. To celebrate and seal the deal, we opened a can of sardines and ate together, and the Congolese sang as John captured it all on video.

In June 1989, we had counted 156 Sunday schools started through ECM training. Up to that point, we had been adding Sunday schools to the list regularly, but with the opening of the Training Center, the numbers would begin to multiply.

We also took Kristi back to her home village, Nkara, to see her family there and to visit her mother's gave. She created quite a commotion there as nearly everyone turned out to see "the baby who wanted to die"—now alive and thriving. The elders brought out elephant tusk horns that had been passed down for generations and were brought out only on special occasions. There were five horns, each of which made a distinct sound, and they were played repetitively in sequence as the people danced in a circle to celebrate seeing Kristi[xiv] again.

ECM ended 1989 with receipts of $44,836.95, which included savings toward a truck for Congo and the construction of the African Leadership Training Center.

At the annual banquet in October 1989, ECM named Floyd Bertsch as International Director in preparation for our return to Congo. Everyone including us and the Bertsches were still serving on a volunteer basis.

Multiplying teachers to reach children—Mission Garizim, 1990

In May 1990, John Henry graduated from high school and worked at Pleasant View Dairy in Highland, IN through the summer. In June, my husband John and I returned to Congo with our adopted Congolese daughter Kristi. John Henry followed us in September.

We receive quite a reception and were able to store the cement we were bringing in the chief's house.

Then we met the workers we had engaged to build our home in advance of our coming. They were less enthusiastic, somewhat embarrassed and quite apologetic. They had heard a rumor that we were not coming, they said, so they had stopped working on our house.

They took us halfway down the hill to the half-completed house. We knew it would be a mud hut with a thatched roof. We had chosen that because we didn't want the first thing we built to be a 'fancy' home for ourselves. However simple by American standards, a cement home with a metal roof would be far above local standards, and we felt it might say to them that our own comfort was our primary concern. However, we had expected a door that would keep out animals that might roam in the night. We knew we would not have glass on the windows, but we expected shutters that could keep out rain, and screen that could keep out malaria-carrying mosquitoes. We were to have none of that for awhile.

I thought I could live with anything in order to serve in Africa, but oh, the assumptions we make without even realizing it! I had expected flat floors. What we found was a mud home built on the hillside without any attempt to flatten out the land first. They kindly and quickly installed a bed for us, but we had to hold on to the edges to keep from falling off because the floor was so slanted. After a few days of feeling like my hip was going out of joint with every step, I called some of the workers in. "This is a dirt floor," I said, gently stomping my feet for emphasis. "Couldn't you take some of this dirt from over there and throw it over here?" I asked.

"Oh, sure, we could easily do that," they assured me.

"OK, would you do it, then?" I asked, barely refraining myself from asking them why on earth they hadn't done it in the first place. That same day they flattened out the dirt floor and I became much more content with our simple home.

We had come to build a training center, but first, we urgently need a place to store the supplies that were on their way. So, John's first project had to be building a storage barn, in Congo called a "depot." There was no electricity and he had no power tools, so everything had to be done by hand. Working with a shovel and a hand saw, square, hammer, hand tin snips, a transit and cement trowels, he and our hired workers built a simple pole-barn like structure with handmade cement posts and PVC pipe bolted on at a slant at the top to form trusses.

They began by creating a little thatch shelter and a cement tray close to the lake where they could get water and mix cement to pour cement posts and to make bricks. By hand, they created a 24' x 24' cement building and put steel roofing on the top. It was finished in two months, just in time to receive and protect our crates of goods. When we arrived back from Kinshasa with those goods, they put the doors on it to make it secure.

Workers with cement posts they are creating by hand for the first depot

We went back to Kinshasa to pick up John Henry in mid-September. We were forced to spend several weeks in Kinshasa, waiting for shipping containers to arrive packed with a tractor, truck and supplies. John and John Henry kept busy by building a wagon for the future work, and by doing several fix-it projects for the Protestant Guest House where we were staying (called CAP, an acronym for "Centre d'Acceuil Protestant). I home schooled Kristi in the CAP dining room, where she began to develop an interest in geography as many guests pointed out their home countries to her on a map. When schooling was finished each day, I worked on the translation of a children's book in Kituba that was eventually published by World Missionary Press of New Paris, IN.

Almost every evening we all took long walks around town. John Henry often commented on the disparity between one side of the street where people lived in luxury and the makeshift huts on the other side, where, as he described it, "people ate mice." Finally, our things arrived and we set off for Mission Garizim. It's a trip of about 500 miles, much of it over very rough, muddy roads.

While in Kinshasa we had met two men who were each independently traveling around the world— Dan Kidd and Skip Nollenberger They asked if they could join us on the trip to the interior and we readily agreed. They later told us that they saw more of the people and culture of Africa on that trip with us than they had in all their previous travels, which we considered quite a compliment.[xv]

What a hullabaloo there was when we arrived on at Lako village just up the hill from the land we had claimed for Mission Garizim! We arrived in the very late afternoon, as the women were returning from their fields carrying heavy loads of produce on their heads. They saw our caravan coming through the tall grass and began to whoop and holler with great joy.

Our mud home

People sometimes ask me what it was like living for six years in a mud hut, so let me describe our home. We made a large, rustic platform for a bed and covered it with a Congolese foam mattress, pretty comfortable when new. Our friend Judy Ericson had sewn pieces of mesh to form a mosquito net to cover the bed. A top sheet lay across the bottom so that we could pull it up if it got chilly during rainy nights. Along the wall in front of our bed, the Africans lashed together small branches to form a platform to keep our suitcases and boxes off the floor. We used the suitcases to organize our clothes and personal belongings. We knew we shared our homes with rats, though we seldom saw them. They liked shiny things, so I would find my shiny scarf impossibly twisted into the thatch roof.[xvi] A cloth curtain hung across our bedroom door for privacy. By Congolese custom, no one would think of entering someone else's bedroom. There was a small window about 18 inches more-or-less 'square' on the front and back of the bedroom, with a wooden shutter that we closed only in the worst of storms.

Workers putting thatch on the roof of our home. You can see the latched walls, which were later packed with mud.

The center room had a door on one side and a small window across from it. There was a wooden table, and straight-back wooden chairs made in Congo, a few plastic stacking shelves we brought with us from the States, and a little platform of sticks lashed together with vine for our water filter.

Central room in our mud hut. The edge of the door to one of the small bedrooms is observable on the right.

Eventually we built a simple desk by placing wood planks over stacked cement blocks.

On the other side of the house were two small bedrooms for Kristi and John Henry. They contained a bamboo bed with a foam pad and a small table for their suitcase. In one of them we also had a kerosene refrigerator. Just outside the door was another platform of sticks lashed together, where we kept a fresh bucket of water for washing our hands. A lot of our living was done outside, most of the time sitting in our "easy" chairs made of wood with seats caned with vines called "nkodi." This was the same vine used to lash together the stick furniture and even our house. To get to the kitchen, you had to go outside and in another door. It had a wood cook stove and more lashed platforms on which our cook Mapiya arranged our few dishes and food items not needing refrigeration. About 20 yards away from the house, there was an outhouse. It was a simple pit latrine covered with a boxlike stool with a hole in the top. John laughed about how he had accomplished cutting a round hole with a straight saw. The outhouse was made of thatch lashed to a stick frame. Like our house, it was covered with a thatch roof. At night we could hear the whir-whir-whir of termites beating their legs on the thatch. We never did figure out what they were doing, but they were not easily disturbed by our watching them.

Soon after our arrival, we had African workers construct a round "sambolo" in front of our home. It was kind of a combination covered patio and outdoor living room, with a thatch roof and thatch lashed up the walls about 2/3 of the way up.

We spent much time there where we could enjoy any breeze available while being out of the hot sun. When our shipping container arrived, it brought us two "comfy" chairs from the States, including our old Lazy Boy recliner.

In February 1991, Floyd and Hildred Bertsch came out to see the developing work. Floyd had become International Director when we went back to Congo in 1990, and Hildred was serving as secretary, both in a volunteer capacity. They helped John put down the foundation to begin construction of what became the African Leadership Training Center. Hildred learned to work the transit and Floyd helped with the heavier work.

Floyd and Hildred Bertsch at Kikwit with Pastor Mawele, who first gave us the idea of establishing Every Child Ministries.

In March of the same year, John began heading up the building of the "bureau" which was to house offices, a library, a two-way radio, and classrooms for training Africans to become "teachers of teachers." This higher-level training was to enable Congolese to become "Master trainers." By equipping many others to train teachers as I had been doing, we figured that the number of Sunday schools could be multiplied. I had been training teachers. The graduates of Garizim would become "Teachers of Teachers."

The Congolese marveled, never having seen a building go up so quickly, thanks to the help of Chuck Daily[xvii] and Ron Smith, who came out to help. Vanessa Slosson also came with them. She helped me teach Kristi, while the men began in earnest building the Training Center. At the end of his time in Congo, Chuck wood burned a rough wooden plaque saying, "To God Be the Glory." Indeed.

John Henry pours cement into the foundation trough that was dug by hand and filled with rocks the women of the area brought from the valley.

John Henry stayed and worked with us for nine months until he went in the army. He was an immense help with the heavy work, so much so that he earned the nickname "Sokoro" (soldier), by which he's been known ever since. (An appropriate title, since he joined the U.S. Army after helping us for nine months.)

While the Training Center was being built, I used the sambolo and the local church up the hill to begin teacher training classes for the Sunday school teachers of the area. Each week, I shared creative teaching ideas and demonstrated the lesson for the coming week. The classes were very well attended, but I suspect that some local leader must have promised them that I would pay them. After a time, they kept insisting that I had promised to do so, although from the beginning I tried to make it very clear that I could not. Whether from pure or mixed motives, however, Sunday schools became very active throughout the area, Bible lessons were flowing to the children, and many were coming to Christ.

On other days, I also used the sambolo as a makeshift local medical clinic. It was all very unofficial, but people discovered we had some medicines and that I was willing to dress tropical sores to keep flies away from them and allow them to heal, and even to dig the egg sacks of chiggers out of children's feet.

One boy came whose feet had all but been destroyed by multiplying chiggers under the skin. He reeked of dead, rotting flesh, and I worked hard to keep my nausea under control so that I could show him the welcoming love of Jesus. Even though I wore gloves to work on his feet, my hands still smelled like decayed flesh. It took repeated washings over several days for the smell to dissipate. However, the boy's feet healed completely and he was soon able to walk normally.

We later started a medical dispensary, first using a mud hut, and later a cement building. Our friend Frank Aldrich drew the blueprints, and John led the workers in building it at the top of the hill. We hired a nurse and a helper.

The clinic provided medical treatment for our own staff and workers quickly and conveniently so that they no longer had to travel to other villages for most of their health care. We also welcomed others who came from villages around us, and some of them from considerable distances. There was a devotional time there to start each day, and students in training at SEC Garizim preached the Gospel there regularly. Nurse Tammy Lape was there just before the official opening, so with the help of another short-termer Kristen Maurer, she thought through what was needed and helped set things up to give efficient service. The dispensary is still functioning as I write this book, but at a reduced level since there is no resident missionary now. Basically it is there for the convenience of ECM's own workers and the students trained at the center, although others are never turned away when they seek help.

In April 1991 we took a short break to meet our first grandson, Jordan Carroll, and attend the marriage of our daughter Carrie to Bill Boehmer. After we returned to Congo around the end of

May, Bill and Carrie followed us for the second leg of their honeymoon. Apparently Carrie had told Bill he could never understand her without experiencing Africa, so the newlywed Boehmers came out to spend the last two weeks of their honeymoon in a mud hut at Mission Garizim. Bill, who is 6'4", stood in the frame of a doorway he was making. It came up to his armpits. "Aren't these doors a little short?" he asked.

Bill, working with our mechanic Mukwa to plane boards for the Training Center

Carrie in the early morning fog, camping along the road on the way to Garizim

Setback-Evacuation

Not all went smoothly. At midnight on September 27, we heard pounding on our door in the middle of the night. Our mechanic had just arrived from Nkara, and he handed us the most unwelcome letter we had ever received. All U.S. citizens were ordered to evacuate Zaire immediately. All expatriates in Kinshasa had already left, and the Kinshasa airport had been closed. Kinshasa was in the hands of the Zairean military. We were supposed to meet a transport plane at Kikwit that day (already past), or at the latest on Saturday. We sat staring at one another by flashlight, too numb to respond. It was a long day's trip to get to Kikwit, so we had to make a decision fast, and practically no background information was given to guide us in the decision.

We had been encouraged by such a good start on the Training Center! The first week had been devoted entirely to prayer and had brought about a wonderful bonding. The two weeks of actual training we had completed had also brought encouraging results, especially the "Life of Victory and Spiritual Warfare" class, where the teaching had resulted in repentance of sin and forgiveness amongst some of the church leaders. Kristin Lund was proving such a help in teaching our daughter Kristi and also in teaching a very popular English class and helping in other ways. With our African staff helping, the beginnings of churches (cell groups) had been planted at Nsim and Lua Nene. The little bands of Christians were being regularly gathered and nourished in Kasangunda and Eyene Molokai. Spirits were good, in spite of the fact that we had overflow classes in three subjects, with people pulling chairs and tree stumps all around the outside edges of our "sambolo" shelter so as to peer in at the windows.

The cement had finally arrived, ready for the floors of our main building to be poured the coming Monday. John had spent the week before putting in the ceilings. The last door had been put on the building that afternoon. Mukwa, our

African mechanic, and his helper Ansete, had ridden double on our one bike 100 miles to the place where our truck had broken down a month before. With parts brought in by Kristin, they had repaired the truck. At long last it appeared that making the cement shell of the Training Center useable was very close—perhaps two weeks of hard work away.

An African-style hut similar to ours had just been completed that morning, ready to welcome Erik and Bambi Carlson, who were expected soon and planned to stay a year. It was hard to believe that with the Training program operating and our permanent building just a grasp away, we were being instructed to leave immediately!

We sent in the night for our mission families to be awakened. As they arrived, we informed them of the situation and we prayed together. Broken, tearful prayers were choked out between soft hymns. It flowed for about half an hour. Every Zairean who prayed, prayed as if we must go and asked God's help and protection for us. We took it as a sign from God confirming that we must leave. Since Monday, people had been telling us of radio reports of widespread rioting and looting in Kinshasa.

John went with some of the men to try to put the kerosene refrigerator and as much of the heavy equipment as possible into the depot, and to disable the tractor. By flashlight, I hastily packed a change of clothes for each of us and gathered our important documents and some family photos. All my American clothes were in Kinshasa, and we were to be evacuated directly to Brazzaville, across the river from Kinshasa in a different country. I walked around our mud hut asking God to bring to mind anything He wanted me to remember. I packed a malaria cure for each of us and wrote letters authorizing Africans to handle various matters for us, and a letter of farewell and explanation to our local church, workers, and Sunday school teachers. I gave instructions for remaining food, soap and medicines to be divided amongst the mission families. Then I laid out extra-generous salaries for each of our sixteen mission workers. All the money that was left, I divided into ten piles on our bed—one for each of the ten African families living on the mission. Then I sat in the darkness and tried to remember if there was anything else I should take. I ran the flashlight around the house, lighting up one precious item after another, all too bulky to take out in hand luggage.

John didn't want to leave the pickup in Kikwit, so we decided we would go to Nkara and try to make radio contact from there. I sent for all the Nkara women and children, knowing they would want to go with us. In their home villages, they could get and receive support as family units.

We needed to leave before morning, in order to avoid drawing crowds, so we sent a messenger to call our local pastor and the foreman of the mission work staff. The women gathered with me in our thatch "living room" and shared verses of encouragement, tears streaming down all our faces. After final songs and prayers, I hugged each of them. I could hardly find a voice to say goodbye.

Then the first rays of dawn began cracking the horizon, and everything began happening at once. Mapiya our cook had warmed up rice and beans for us to eat, several people needed last minute instructions which we tried to give between bites, the handbags were going out the door, the Nkara people were being packed in the truck along with their handbags, cooking pots and chickens. Our local pastor arrived, and soon we were gathered in a semi-circle around the truck, holding hands with our beloved African family, offering final prayers with broken hearts.

It was a six-hour ride to Nkara over a road John particularly despised, but we only got stuck once, and that time, not too badly. On the road, however, we had a problem with the radiator overheating. After it cooled off for about 30 minutes, we put our drinking water into the radiator and John drove in low gear to make the engine run cooler. He had not been underway long after that, when we heard a loud "bang" and the rear window of the truck suddenly burst, scattering pieces of glass on our backs and laps. At first I thought we were being shot at, but apparently a manioc sifter had jammed down by the glass, so when the truck twisted on the uneven road, the pressure was too much. John shouted, "Is everyone OK?" Being assured that no one had been cut, he yelled, "Brush the glass off! I'm not stopping!"

At Nkara, we made radio contact only to hear them say over and over that all MAF planes were already in Brazzaville, and all remaining families must go to Kikwit. There was no time left to do that, and the truck was in no condition to make the trip. No one acknowledged our calls, but suddenly we heard a plane overhead. "That's it!" we said, jumping into the truck and racing up to the airstrip, where we boarded immediately. It was David Law, an independent missionary pilot.

He said they were holding the last plane out of Kikwit for us. He had not answered us because he did not want anyone to know his location so there would be no unpleasant surprises when he landed.

After a fifteen-minute trip, we arrived in Kikwit, to be greeted by rows of French soldiers with automatic weapons and grenade launchers in ready position. A huge Zairean crowd looked on from a distance. We were immediately transferred to a large French military transport plane. The French military had seized control of the airport for evacuation purposes. Other than military and evacuees, the place was deserted. The inside of the airport, were told, had been totally demolished by rioters and looters.

At Brazzaville, there were even more troops all over the airport. We were escorted to a State Dept. official who expedited our paperwork. Soon we were outside with a group of about forty other Americans, including several missionaries we knew. We eventually joined about 400 evacuees in one of several centers where we were being gathered. The food line was long, but we were treated with kindness and efficiency, and soon were enjoyed a barbecue and being hugged by other missionaries who had been concerned about our isolation and had been praying for us. We were tired and dirty, but lying down for a couple of hours on pieces of carpet on the ground helped a lot.

There, as we compared experiences with others, we began to realize the extent of the desolation. Most stores and businesses had been destroyed, even the bakery that provides bread for the 4.5 million people who then lived in Kinshasa[xviii]. There was no fuel and little food in the city. What manioc (the staple food) could be brought into the city from the country had increased in price 8 times overnight--to a price impossible for the average citizen. In Kikwit, too, all the stores had been looted.

John signed a promissory note to pay for our trip home. About 10 p.m. we were taken to the airport and loaded onto a charter flight to Washington, D.C. Only 54 hours after we received the evacuation notice, we were at the Bertsch's home in Indiana, where we called loved ones to assure them of our safety.

We did not know at the time if we would ever be able to return, but although it appeared that the hosts of Satan were trying to destroy the nation of Zaire and the work of God there, the story was not over yet. After a few months, Mission Aviation Fellowship convened a meeting of missions serving in Zaire to discuss possible return, assuring us that they were there "for the long haul." We could say the same. The ECM annual report for 1991 was entitled, "Open Doors." Our ministry account had been wiped out, so we began rebuilding support funds and returned to Zaire in early February, 1992.

Developing Master Trainers

The program came to be called SEC—an acronym for the French name, "Spécialité en Education Chrétienne" (Specialty in Christian Education). In English we called it the "African Leadership Training Center." It was later expanded to Kinshasa for several years, so in Congo it came to be known as SEC Garizim and SEC Kin.

The first class, graduating in 1992, was taught by me and by Pastor Mayele, whom we had taught at Nkara. After graduation we had sent him to the CEF Institute in Switzerland to prepare him for becoming a member of our staff. That first year, we trained those we intended to become ECM's own staff, trainers for the SEC program in the future.

As people completed the SEC program and graduated, some of them became ECM staff. Those who did not work for ECM often became heads of the Christian Education Departments of their denominations.

I began training classes for the Master Trainer level in the unfinished classrooms as the men continued to work on finishing the building. From the beginning, those in training were assigned villages all around the center at Mission Garizim where they worked alongside local village churches to create Sunday schools for children and sought to implement the methods and ideas they were learning during the week.

Bible School & Women's School

In the beginning, we also had a Bible School, called FEBT (**feh**-beh-tay), short for the French "Faculté d'Education Biblique et Théologique), led by Pastor Kongolo. It was much needed when we started it, but after the graduation of the first class, some of the church groups had started their own Bible schools, so we dropped that program to concentrate exclusively on our specialty— Christian education, specially for children. However, even though only one class graduated, we are gratified to hear that the churches are appreciating the ministries of those graduates. Only one class, but those graduates will offer a whole lifetime of service to Congo! As I write, I recently saw on Facebook a picture of a new church building being constructed in Kikwit by one of these graduates.

While the Bible school was running, we also had a women's program called ECOFEM (Ecole des Femmes) for the wives of students who for one reason or another were not taking the full program. Bambi Carlson was a huge help with the women.

Erik and Bambi Carlson

It was a challenging program, and sometimes discouraging for Bambi, since many of the women had little education and a very limited world view. I remember one time when the women had seen soap made in blue plastic tubs. When the men went to buy the tubs, all they could find were red tubs. Some of the women insisted that they could not make soap in a red tub. It had to be blue, since that was the way they had seen it done, and they had to stir it right to left, not left to right. Bambi was hard put to convince them that it would also work in a red tub!

One of Bambi's most popular ministries was teaching the women some simple group line-dance steps, similar to choreography. Bambi translated "Jesus, King of Kings and Lord of Lords" and some other songs into Kituba and the women proudly sang and performed it with their dance steps at their graduation. When FEBT was closed, there was no longer any reason for the women's ministry, so it, too was closed and the Christian education program continued.

It is that for which Mission Garizim became widely known. Sixteen years afterwards, I also visited one of their churches in Kikwit and found Mama Pasteur Ntima enthusiastically working with the women and children of the church, and thanking God for what Bambi taught her in ECOFEM.

Bambi's husband Erik worked hard helping John finish the veranda on the training center, and getting an airstrip started for the mission. Both of them helped teach Kristi. They were with us for eleven months and helped in so many ways with the development of Garizim.

Top-The Carlsons, John and me officiating at Garizim's first graduation, Middle-Graduates and official guests parading into the ceremony Next page-The expanded depot on the left, Training Center, outhouses in the foreground

Garizim Growing

John continued building Mission Garizim, including doubling the size of the depot, building a permanent medical clinic, finishing the airstrip that Erik Carlson had done so much work on, and building what was supposed to become our home—not out of mud, but cement, with a metal roof and lots of ventilation.

After the first class graduated, several of the graduates joined the teaching team, and I also continued teaching. When John installed three solar panels on the Training center building, I was able to use a laptop to create lessons and other literature. We printed it there on an old dot-matrix printer, and sold the literature in the bookstore there, and in the villages during evangelistic trips.

My weekly training class for local Sunday school teachers continued. For one series of lessons, I decided to experiment with a new, more active approach. Following the idea of expository preaching that covers one part of Scripture verse-by-verse, I choose the book of Jonah, then divided it into small segments. While I had previously published a single lesson on the entire book of Jonah with Child Evangelism Fellowship, this series on Jonah was divided into sixteen lessons! Each lesson was divided into about four sections, each very short—often only one or two verses.

Whereas previously I had insisted on teachers reading and retelling a summary of the lesson, in this case I encouraged them to read the Scripture directly from the Bible. The only exception was

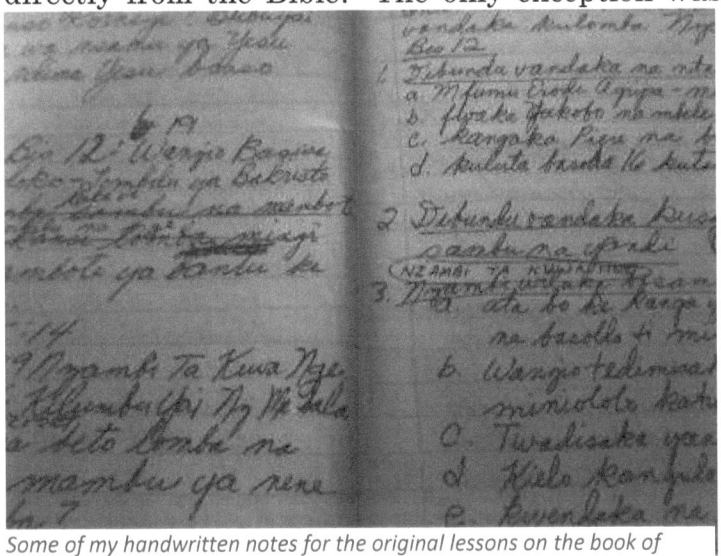

Some of my handwritten notes for the original lessons on the book of Jonah

the long prayer Jonah prayed while in the belly of the fish. We summarized that. Then, with each section, the teacher would ask questions about what had just been read, lead the children in acting out what they had read, and finally lead them in singing and dancing to that same teaching. The experiment went over very well. The teachers found the lessons easy to follow and to teach, the children enjoyed them immensely, and afterward they really knew the book of Jonah! Those lessons later became the pattern for much of our teaching.

When Money Loses its Value

The thing that affected us most during this time was the rapid and severe devaluation of the money. The leaders of the time felt that if the country needed money, they could just print it. At its height, money was losing value virtually by the hour. We had to keep all our funds invested in goods that we knew would sell well because they were universally needed or desired—things like soap, dried fish, salt, sugar, school notebooks and pens, canned tomato sauce, canned sardines, etc. Any money kept in cash for even a few days lost almost all its value.

At that time, our support was also dangerously low. By eating local foods, we were able to live.

However, our support also had to cover the cost of all the ministries we were doing, and that was the difficult part. The staff and workers, who had to pay school fees for their children, found life extremely difficult. Our little "canteen" (store) where we sold necessary items to them was essential, because such items became almost impossible to get as merchants were running out of funding and the shelves of local stores becoming bare. The "canteen" was also a help to us, the only way we could retrieve funds at a somewhat current rate.

However, as time went on, it became more and more difficult for our workers to purchase anything. Of course, with conditions so difficult, they were crying out for raises in pay, but we, too, were suffering under the reality of constant devaluation, and it was utterly impossible for us to give raises.

The government did not pay its workers or its military for many months or even years at a time, so their employees began to look for creative ways to get money, and the few of us who had some outside connections became prime targets.

In the last days of Mobutu's power, we entertained a constant flow of public officials desperately looking for some "infraction" with which they could charge us so that they could fine us and get money. What at first had been primarily officials looking for funds for their year-end holiday celebration (their "bonne fête"), it later became a constant problem. As we look back, we can't explain how God got us through, but somehow He did.

Garizim Graduates

Several classes graduated from Garizim while we were there in the 1990's. One of them, Pastor ("Pasteur" in French) Munda became the head pastor of a district in the extreme southern part of the Bandundu Province. He trained many teachers and helped many churches of his area establish Sunday schools for children, also reaching across the Congo border into Angola. The villages in that part of Angola also speak Kituba as they do in Bandundu, since the colonial powers did not observe tribal boundaries, but "cut up" tribes, assigning them to different countries. Pastor Munda is still on staff with ECM as I write this book.

During that time, too, one of the pygmies came for training. He had been evangelized when Kiketi and Munguba went into the rain forest on a mission trip. (That story is told in more detail in my first book.) Mweta attended the African

Leadership Training Center at Mission Garizim and graduated to go back and encourage and teach his own pygmy people to reach children.

John and I met with Mweta again at Congo's 2019 Reunion in Kikwit. Pastor Munguba from Garizim is at the right.

Most teachers and trainers in Congo were men, because the daily chores of most women to provide for their family's living consume virtually all their time and energy.

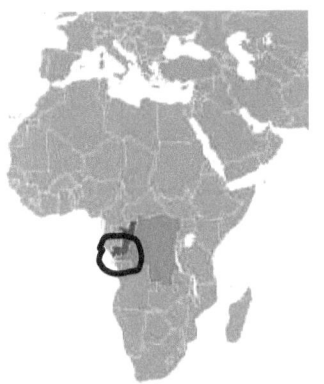

The smaller country to the left is Congo-Brazzaville, the larger one to the right is "our" Congo—DRCongo, formerly Zaire. The circle shows the territory of the Kingdom of Kongo that the first European explorers encountered in the 1400's, covering parts of four modern nations.

However, a few women did attend the Training center as well. One of the first was Esther Mahoungou, from the Republic of Congo across the river from Kinshasa. Congo-Brazza, as it is commonly called, is a separate country, and the similar name often creates confusion when people talk about Congo. "Our" Congo, called Zaire when we were there, is the Democratic Republic of Congo, colonized by the Belgians. "Esther's" Congo, across the river from "ours", is the Republic of Congo, colonized by the French, commonly called Congo-Brazzaville for its capital. Again, as in the case of Munda serving on the southern boundary, the Kituba language reaches across the border into Congo Brazzaville because all the people, before colonial times divided them, were part of the Kingdom of Kongo.

After graduation, Esther went back to Brazzaville and helped about 30 churches start Sunday schools. In the years of turmoil, we lost track of Esther, and were later saddened to learn that she was killed in one of Congo's wars. ECM lost track of those churches. In 2016, we made a new start in Brazzaville, but had to drop efforts there when our new trainer neglected to give reports.[xix]

Other graduates became the heads of Christian education in their respective denominations and were in a position to promote with all their churches the ideas that children are important and that the church needs to teach them God's Word and reach them for Christ. Since many parents are illiterate or barely literate, this is even more important in Congo than it is in the U.S., where families can, if they choose to do so, read the Bible together.

In 1996, five classes had graduated from the Training Center. We were multiplying Master Trainers who were in turn training other teachers in many different areas. The number of Sunday schools where children were being taught God's Word and won to Christ was increasing rapidly. Our vision of a Sunday school in every village of the Bandundu Province seemed very reachable, and the Garizim graduates had even reached out into two other countries in at least a small way.

Change of Leadership in Congo—Mobutu is Out and Kabila is In

In 1996 Laurent Kabila's soldiers began a march of destruction across the country seeking to oust President-dictator Mobutu Sese Seko.[xx] Most missions in their path were stripped bare, the soldiers removing doors, windows, and even toilets.

We were at Garizim when we heard that Kabila's forces had arrived only 20 miles from the mission. Garizim was in danger--all of us there, and everything we had worked to build up. We considered staying, and hiding in the forest if necessary, along with our staff and workers. We were willing to do so if our presence would encourage them.

However, they felt that we would attract immediate attention from the soldiers, putting their lives in greater danger. We immediately radioed Mission Aviation Fellowship. They quickly sent a plane, and we left with only a few of our belongings, leaving the staff to hide as many of the mission goods as they could in the forest around the mission.

With the country in such turmoil and the radio hidden in the forest, we had no communication with the staff for awhile. We were unable to get any funds to them for a whole year. We assumed they would be forced to close the Training Center, and we wrote such in our newsletters.

Were we ever amazed and thrilled later on to learn that after that first band of soldiers passed, taking only some manual typewriters, our personal supply of canned meat, and our barrels of fuel, that our people emerged from the forest and continued ministry at the Training Center. Life was hard going for them, working a whole year with no salary, but somehow, they survived and continued the work. They explained later that they knew we would make up their salaries when we could. It was our strong relationship with them that God used to carry us all through that difficult time.

Meanwhile, some of our people had taken the big truck out on evangelism. They heard that the soldiers were at Garizim, realized that the valleys easily echoed sound over long distances, and that the truck would be a prize for the soldiers. So they turned the truck off and pushed it by hand off into the bushes, covering it with brush so that no one passing would easily recognize it. The truck was saved for future ministry through their creativity and hard work.

Later one of the graduates, Kalema, was named as Congo Director. He moved to Kinshasa and built on the work I had started there in the seminars I had done in the 1980's. Sunday schools in the city tended to be much larger than those in the villages, some of them reaching hundreds of children, but also faced logistical problems resulting from crowding. To make the situation even more challenging for Sunday school teachers there, pastors often insisted on having Sunday school for children at the same time as the adult worship services, blasting the service at full volume through loud speakers.

Where was the vision in the midst of the troubles?

Of course, those churches who did reach out to children prior to ECM's intervention had begun in the big churches of the city. However, at one point, several ECM staff members did surveys of the work of churches in Kinshasa amongst children. They found that even in the capital city, a little fewer than half the churches still had any program at all to reach children. Most welcomed ECM's training and were eager to start Sunday schools with ECM's guidance and training.

After 1997, Congo was embroiled in many political disturbances and wars. We were unable to live there for some years. In 1998, the staff at Garizim underwent a time of harassment from the military. Apparently someone had given them false reports, claiming that we might be looking for valuable minerals there. Soldiers came to Garizim three times that Spring, interrogating the staff at great length. They demanded to know what wealth we missionaries were looking for there. The remote location seemed to arouse their suspicions. Why did we "have" to build the mission there and only there? During the questioning, one drunken soldier kept pounding his loaded rifle on the ground around the feet of some of our leaders. They thought for sure it would discharge, but God protected them, and the rifle never fired a shot.

One night, the Garizim leaders also became aware that the soldiers were lurking around outside their windows, eavesdropping. They didn't hear much except singing and praying. All buildings were inspected thoroughly. Of course, nothing was found, because we weren't hiding anything. The soldiers threatened to beat the staff with whips and confiscate the truck, fill it with soldiers and send it into battle. But the truck was not running, and after investigation, they admitted they must have been given a false report. The radio was confiscated, and the airstrip was disabled, but staff actually rejoiced at that, knowing it would not be used to bring troops in to fight in the area.

The Training Center at Mission Garizim continued developing Master Trainers, but things proceeded at a slower pace. We had not forgotten about the vision of a Sunday school in every village. In fact, since our workers were then in Kinshasa, we had added the phrase, "and in every neighborhood of the cities." However, we realized that we were not personally going to be able to pursue that vision as rapidly or as fully as we had planned. Our hearts were still there, but we didn't know when or even if we'd ever be able to return.

We had lived for a very short time in the bare shell of our new cement home when these events happened. There had been neither funds nor time to paint it, decorate it, or build furniture beyond the basic necessities. To make best use of the facilities God had given us, we allowed the staff to divide our home. One part became a staff home, the other part a student dormitory.

Teachers' Resource Libraries

Almost from the beginning, Garizim had become a source from which we loaned teaching materials to the churches of the area. This enabled Sunday school lessons, pictures when available, and visualized verses painstakingly created by hand one by one, to be used over and over. We estimated that some of the loaned materials lasted as long as twelve years. This made the time invested in creating them feel worthwhile. Our daughter Carrie and some others who visited the mission helped in the creation of materials.

In those days, the Mennonites had translated and mimeographed about five different books of lessons from Scripture Press. We bought them by the carton from their bookstore in Kintambo (a neighborhood in Kinshasa). We visualized verses on posterboard bought in country and matched them with pictures we had brought from the U.S.

whenever possible, putting them into packets. Teachers walked to Garizim for distances of over twenty miles to receive and exchange the packets. As Congo's troubles went on, that bookstore eventually closed, and Sunday school materials in Kituba became virtually impossible to find for several years. This remained the case until after we stepped out of the International Directorship position and were free to concentrate our efforts on the needs of Congo once again.

During the years we spent in the States in the 80's, I had developed a Training Manual for Sunday School teachers. In 1998, an anonymous Christian group donated $40,000, which enabled us to print the manual in large quantities in four major African languages—Kituba, Lingala, French, and Tshiluba. Then in 1999, I helped to develop the website www.teachingforafrica.com, offering teaching and training helps for African churches. Although we knew most of the Bandundu Province where we had served did not have internet access, we hoped it might reach major African cities. This resulted in contacts with numerous African countries.

In May 2000, one of our trainers, Pastor Mwamba, was arrested in Congo. He had not realized that because of the war there, a new law had been issued forbidding assembly without written permission of the government. So when he gathered Sunday school teachers to be trained at Itere-Ngienkung, soldiers appeared to arrest him and take him to the head of security in the area. There he was harassed and great sums of money were demanded from him. Some of the teachers became frightened and left. Mwamba decided to take a humble, soft approach. He remembered that the Bible says, "A soft answer turns away wrath" (Proverbs 25:15) and "God resists the proud, but gives grace to the humble" (1 Peter 5:5). So he asked forgiveness of his captors for not getting a permit. The Bible principles worked. The attitude of his captors quickly changed. After a short time he was dismissed after paying a token fine, and with permission to complete the seminar. The training continued with fifteen teachers who remained, and as a result, five new Sunday schools were established in the area. By August, 2000, we had recorded 1,456 Sunday schools we knew had been started through ECM training.

2. Ghana & Character Building from the Bible 1999

When we realized that we would not be immediately able to remain as personally involved in Congo as we had planned, we began to think about sharing our time with other mission efforts. Through the 'teachingforafrica.com' website, we had received letters from several African countries inviting us to begin ECM's program there. John's expertise is in construction and he was not inclined to learn another new language, so we considered invitations from countries where English was the basic language. We chose to make a trip to Ghana in 1999. Alan Cox, then chair of the ECM Board, went with John and me. The plan was to check out the needs and missionary opportunities, while also presenting three teacher training seminars.

The seminars were well attended and the teachers seemed appreciative of fresh ideas, but we found that while Sunday school was a fresh, new and exciting idea in Congo, it was an old idea in Ghana, an idea that some even publicly ridiculed. It was evident that Sunday school was not going to be the method by which Ghanaian families could be reached with the Gospel.

In fact, Ghana seemed filled with many small churches, as evidenced by a multitude of church signs on many street corners. Although the seminars seemed to help the churches, I could easily see that we were not by this means entering new territory as was the case in Congo.

However, God showed us some new ways to reach children in Ghana. After the first seminar, we put on staff Evelyn Antwi, who received the top grade on the final exam. Evelyn became a good friend and I enjoyed teaching with her. After another trip to Ghana in 2000 to train a small beginning staff, Evelyn and I were visiting a school and talking with the school head mistress (principal). We had discussed the possibility of bringing out summer teams to help build the ministry. Suddenly the Lord implanted in my mind a basic plan for public school ministry. It was to be called "Character Building from the Bible" and was to consist of Bible stories showing positive character traits, with Bible verses to accompany the lesson. Of course, Jesus was the only One who ever fulfilled perfectly every good character trait. It was so clear that I spoke as if we had researched the idea and planned it out carefully.

In fact, we had absolutely nothing on paper, no prepared lessons, nothing. We had only an idea that I believe God placed into my mind at that very moment. The head mistress loved the idea and accepted our proposal. I wrote the first lessons and prepared visuals. We recruited the first summer team for 2001. John also helped as timekeeper, since it was important not to overstay our welcome and cut into the classroom teachers' time.

We made the lessons available to the teachers in advance so they could study them. We also recruited a Ghanaian teaching partner for each American. Meeting together for a few days before beginning the teaching, we discussed both the lesson and the methods to be used. In small groups, each set of teaching partners decided on some kind of active student participation for each main point of the Bible lesson. I created songs and taught songs to go along with the lessons.

From the first day, Character Building from the Bible was a roaring success. Active teaching methods that not only allowed for, but actually encouraged student movement and participation seemed to be new in Ghana. The students

Lois Pope invites students to come to Christ.

absolutely loved it, and most of the teachers seemed just as excited.

After our first year's ministry, we were surprised and thrilled to receive an official letter from the Ghana Education Service thanking us for the program and inviting ECM to take it into all the schools of Ghana.[xxi] Oh, how I wished we had the resources to do that! That was one of many times when I longed for God to enable us to build Every Child Ministries bigger, stronger, and faster. In reality, we did not have the strength to fully implement the program even throughout the Accra[xxii] district alone, let alone the other districts of Ghana.

However, we renewed our commitment to do as much as we possibly could. Every summer we took the program into three new areas. We tried to recruit teaching partners who could continue the ministry on a monthly basis, with a small stipend of encouragement, after the American team left. We found that bringing an American team to teach opened many doors. No school that we approached in those years refused to allow the program to enter.

Since we were teaching large classes and going from one school to another, we were not always privileged to see the results of our work beyond the students' responses to questions. However, we learned that in one location, a group of students had previously banded together and robbed another student. When the ECM team presented the lesson on "Truthfulness, Not Deceit," some of them received Christ and then became convicted about what they had done. They confessed their sin, returned what they had stolen, and asked forgiveness. The teacher reported the incident to the headmaster, and "Character Building from the Bible" quickly gained a good reputation in the district.

We were never restricted in our presentation of the Gospel, so we worked hard to make the Biblical way of salvation clear. We did not think it wise to ask for a public testimony like raising hands or coming forward, but we made it clear how students could receive Jesus as their Savior on their own at any time. We asked them, if they made this decision, to write their name on a scrap of paper along with the words, "I took Jesus." The next week, they were to slip those notes to any of our team at any convenient time.

Many students did so, and I have in my office today a collage made of many scraps of paper, each saying "I took Jesus," and some with a more detailed testimony and the name of a student. That collage is one of my greatest treasures, and has been an encouragement to me many times and a reminder that our work bore eternal fruit.

Over the next 11 years, we took many teams each summer[xxiii] and taught thousands of children in the school ministry at both public and private schools. The teachers varied in their ability and experience, but all made a positive contribution. One teacher I remember distinctly was Abigail Kean. Not only was she an excellent teacher herself, but when her teaching partner was presenting his part, Abby would follow him showing such keen interest that it drew the students into the lesson even more. It was a habit I wanted all of our teachers to emulate.

I remember another teacher who introduced the students to some new action-type songs that they loved and remembered for a long time.

The vast majority of students were very enthusiastic. Only a very few Muslim and Jehovah's Witness students opted out, and often they sat in the back or quietly on the side, doing other work. Some from groups like this attended but refused to participate. Teachers asked me what they should do about this. Should they try to force students to participate?

I quickly nixed that idea, telling them that "Someone convinced against his will is of the same opinion still." I knew that insistence on participation could lead to protests from angry parents, and I really did believe in freedom of religion. I suggested that those within earshot were still being exposed to the Gospel, and that was a good thing, since then they would know the way of salvation and would be able to accept it later, when God might show them their need of Christ. Since they were not interrupting the teaching of the other children, I suggested we allow such children to just sit quietly, knowing that they would still be taking in the Word.

We were surprised that one of the schools where we ended up teaching said in a sign above the door, "Muslim School." We learned it began as a Muslim school but was now a public school. I am sure that the Good News came into many Muslim homes, however, through ECM's "Character Building from the Bible" program.

The people in control in the Ghana Education Service (GES) changed every few years according to the political party in power. The program later became less feasible when the GES stipulated that all religious teaching had to be done on one certain day of the week. Since we had a limited number of teachers, there was no way they could teach in one day all the schools that desired the program. This severely limited the school ministry. The program was also dropped in some areas for financial reasons[xxiv], but continues in a few areas, where it continues to bring children to Jesus and build them up in the Word of God.

Leslie Bailey teaching with Benard Fianku

I later realized that good character is needed everywhere, so I eventually translated all the character-building lessons into Kituba for use in

Congo Sunday schools and later on a kids' radio program that I developed there.

3. Seeing Street Children—Ghana (1999)

My eyes were so focused on village children during our first two terms in Congo that I hardly recognized other groups of children that Sunday Schools might not reach. God began to call homeless street children to my attention when we went to Ghana for an exploratory trip in 1999. We visited a work that Pastor Larry Lamina of Handivangelism was doing in downtown Accra with physically handicapped adults. Many of them were living on the streets of the downtown area.

Pastor Alex Boamah was showing us around, and seeing street children, he asked if we'd like to see how they slept at night. We said, "Sure." Alex told us we'd need to wait until after midnight, so we stayed up that night. Alex picked us up around 1 a.m. and we headed downtown. We passed a few people sleeping in the doorways of businesses that were closed for the night. When we turned into the parking lot adjacent to the central train station, we were shocked. People were lying everywhere on cloths on the ground. There were so many that we realized they could not all be waiting for the next train. A few were mothers sleeping alongside their children, but there were also many children sleeping all alone, all by themselves.

Alex explained that the homeless gathered there to sleep because that parking lot was sheltered by walls and there was a train station guard on duty, which reduced the danger of being attacked by thieves. I was shocked to learn that they had to pay nightly to stay there. It was only a few cents, but a considerable amount to someone who was dependent on begging for each day's food.

We discovered that when it rains, all the people sleeping in the parking lot have to crowd together under the comparative shelter of the train station waiting area. There is insufficient shelter there for people to lie down there, so they have to stand. On occasion children had drowned when they fell asleep standing up and fell into the muddy water collecting around the cement base of the station.

Suddenly I began to see street children in a new light. We began a street children's fellowship soon afterwards. Sunday afternoon, we learned, was the least busy time for street kids. Begging, which was their main way of making a living, was very slow at that time. So, we arranged for a pastor's wife, Felicia Annan, to join Alex and Benard Fianku, a worker recommended by Alex, to teach them every Sunday afternoon. Whenever we were in Accra, we would join them, as would the American teaching teams that came out every summer for the "Character Building from the Bible" ministry.

The American teams could not teach without translation, for the street children had never been to school, hence, had never learned English, except for "Me hungry. Give me money." The teams, however, were very effective in leading group games and dances. Oh, how the children welcomed that relief from their dreary lives!

One street child was called Saddam. It was years before I discovered his real name was Abdul, and he was called Saddam Hussein on the streets because he was so tough. Saddam was about three years old when we first met him. He lived alone, as far as we could tell, there in the parking lot. To beg during the day, he darted in and out of dangerous, busy traffic on main roads. I later bragged, when telling audiences about Every Child Ministries, that I bet I was the only one there who had actually held Saddam Hussein on my lap.[xxv]

Another girl, Aishetu, had active AIDS. She had open sores all over her body. I thought twice about holding her on my lap, but I decided to trust God to protect me. I couldn't shun her while teaching the children that Jesus touched a leper. It was too important to demonstrate the love of Jesus to her. I just did my best to use lots of hand sanitizer and antiseptic wipes as soon as I was out of sight of the children, also changed my clothes and showered immediately as soon as I got back to our apartment at Haven of Hope. Sadly, Aishetu later died of AIDS, but not before opening her heart to Jesus. I did not contract the disease and am still HIV negative.

Felicia, a pastor's wife, was a wonderful teacher. The children loved her. She was a champion at making the best use of whatever materials she had. Someone sent her a coloring book and some crayons. But what was one coloring book amongst 50 or 60 children? She found a creative solution. She held the coloring book on her lap, and called one child at a time to come and color a small portion, even while she continued teaching or reviewing the lesson.

Many of the street children turned to Christ. Sadly, they were not welcomed in the churches of the area. The general population of the area was much better off and did not want to ruin their "respectability" by associating with street children. The general attitude seemed to be that it was their own fault they were on the street. In fact, a few of the older youth may have chosen the street, but most found themselves forced there because they simply had no other place to go. ECM workers did their best to welcome them and to disciple them after coming to Christ.

After some time, I realized that the lessons developed specially for school ministry could be very useful elsewhere as well. We used them later very effectively in the street ministry.

As we got to know the street children, it pained us to teach them, hug them, give them one meal, and then leave them to sleep alone on the street. We began to think what it might be like if we were develop a children's home. The best situation would be to live with loving parents in their own home. Since that was not possible for so many of them, the second best seemed to be to try to provide a substitute home and family with a loving Christian atmosphere. In the next chapter, you will read about the development of Haven of Hope.

Since God had opened our eyes to see street children and their needs, we encouraged our Congo staff to also begin to work with street children in Kinshasa. Our offices were near a market area called Binza UPN, and we found that there were many street children there. They slept under the makeshift booths in the open market area and under trees at the University. (The U in UPN.) We designated two staff members to befriend them, and soon a street fellowship had developed, with about 60 children, mostly teenage boys, attending regularly.

One of the things that touched my heart deeply was the comment of one of the street kids in Congo that before ECM workers came to "their" market, no one had ever spoken to them as human beings in a kind or friendly manner. It was only "Hey, kid, carry this bag." They said the friendly, accepting, caring manner of our staff was the reason they came to the street fellowship, and that eventually led them to Jesus. I was never prouder of our workers, and never so thrilled to be counted as one of them.[xxvi]

4. Seeing Homeless Children-- Haven of Hope, Ghana (2001)

Early into ECM's street ministry in Ghana, our hearts began to ache when, after sharing the Word with the children, and giving them a meal, and playing games with them, and holding them on our laps, and sometimes receiving clinging hugs, we had to say goodbye, knowing that night would soon fall and the children would sleep again alone on a plastic sack that someone had discarded. We realized that for some, we were all the family they had. Ours were the only kind words they might hear all week, our teaching their only guidance in the tough life people lived on the streets.

We began to dream of a substitute home where loving Christians might live with these children and at least to some degree take the place of caring parents. We began to dream about what it might be like if there was a place where they might receive Biblically-based guidance every day and in every situation that they faced. A safe place, free from robbers, rapists and child traffickers. A place where every child would be valued and encouraged.

Our thoughts seesawed back and forth between the urgent need for such a home, and the immensity of the work and fund-raising that would be involved, as well as the long-term commitment we would be making to children who entered there. Like virtually every project ECM has undertaken, it was a huge leap into the realm of the impossible. We knew that only God could bring together all that would be needed, but as we prayed, our confidence began to grow that He indeed would help us. One of the key factors at that time was talking to two friends of the ministry, Sharyl Albright and her sister Lana Foster. As they followed the developing street ministry, their hearts and faith were a couple steps ahead of us, and as we talked, they greatly encouraged us to go ahead. The children must have a home, and God was going to enable ECM to provide it.

First, we needed land

We asked the Ghanaian pastor friend who had introduced us to the street children, Alex Boamah, to begin looking for a property ECM might purchase, where we could build a home for street children who were not with their families. Alex looked for quite a while before he found the 8-acre property that is now Haven of Hope.

John and Pastor Alex bargained with a local chief, an attorney worked on the official papers, and ECM purchased that property for $16,000 from a local chief in 2001 on a 99-year lease. Given ECM's budget, that was a ginormous amount at the time. Construction began on April 1, 2002 with Dick Bashore, Bob and Denise Elder, Bob Eriks, and my husband John, along with a crew of hired Ghanaian laborers. The weather was unusually torrid, so much so that Bob described it as going to work on the face of the sun. The workers had constructed a 12'x12' thatch shelter. Although it was still hot under its shade, it provided a very much welcomed relief from the sun. Dick Bashore had the honor of officially laying the first cement block on April 5, 2002. By August, the shell of the first dormitory and adjoining bath house was completed.

Immediately, foundations were poured for a dining hall and first staff housing unit.

Haven of Hope opens—oh, joy!

I was not able to be there for the official opening, but I was in Ghana shortly before that, and we arranged to take a load of the street kids out to the location to see what would soon become their new home. The shell of the building was nearly completed, but there was no furniture. We sat on the bare terrazzo floor, and I remember one of the boys rubbing his tummy on the floor as if to say, "I've never felt anything this nice before." Indeed.

What a joy it was to see the reaction of the children!

There was an outside toilet and bath house with four American sit-down type toilets and four showers. Another team consisted of Lana Foster, Nicol Sobol and Andy Munson. They came in the summer of 2002, helped with the street ministry, played with the children at Haven of Hope, and did some finishing work and painting on the bath house.

On November 23, 2002, children moved from their nomadic existence on the streets into their new home. Bernard Fianku, who was directing the street ministry at the time, led a small program in the unlandscaped yard just outside that first building, to welcome them. ECM hired women to act as "mothers," caring for the children's basic needs. That night, the children all slept on a bed, most of them for the first time in their lives. Girls slept in their own room at one end of the home, boys in their own room at the other end, with the mothers' room and an all-purpose room in-between.

How exciting it was for the children to spend their first Christmas at Haven of Hope! There had been little opportunity to celebrate when they had been living on the street. The report received from the home said the children had celebrated with "Christmas decorations." We laughed when we got the picture of the event. The "decorations" were party hats with ruffles made by the mothers and sunglasses for the children! They also received a few simple plastic toys, and a meal of mutton complete with soft drinks was prepared to make the day extra-festive.

The following February (2003), a well was dug at the home giving the children fresh, safe, drinking water. No longer did it need to be purchased from the nearby village.

Now we're just like other children—we go to school!

Virtually all the children had never been to school, so for the first several months, the mothers taught them the basics of reading, writing, and understanding letters and numbers. The children drew what they were learning on small lap chalkboards.

Then, when the new term began, they all proudly donned school uniforms ECM had sewn for them, the mothers packed lunches in little plastic tubs, and they marched off to the nearby village school. After coming to Haven of Hope, beginning school was certainly the most exciting day of their young lives. Now the children felt they were just like other kids. It was a good feeling.

At that time, cooking and eating were both done under a small makeshift shelter with a metal roof. The next building to go up was a combination kitchen and dining room (completed July 2003), with two small rooms on one end that have served a variety of purposes over the years.

Haven of Hope grows

Then in 2003, the walls began to go up on the first of three guest housing apartments, the last of which also housed the home's first library. That work continued through 2011, even as other construction was also going on.

In 2004 the first school "block", as a group of classrooms is called in Ghana, was built to provide high-quality Christian education for the children of Haven of Hope. We had tried to send them to local schools, but found that often the teachers refused to teach unless paid extra (beyond their salaries) by the students. So we decided to create our own school where we would also teach them of Jesus. The school was basically to meet the needs of the Haven of Hope kids, but of course, we admitted children from the surrounding community as well.

At about the same time, our son John Henry came to Ghana to install solar power along with my husband John. John Henry remembers that it was very hot, so one day his dad asked a worker to hold an umbrella over his head as he welded the solar frames so that he wouldn't get "cooked from both sides." He particularly remembers that when he flipped the circuit breaker to turn on the lights for the first time at Haven of Hope, there was a great roar from the home. The kids were all cheering, whooping, hollering at the tops of the lungs. The mothers came out dancing, waving towels in the air.

John Henry also help to install playground equipment. The children had never before seen swings or a slide, so after setting up the equipment, John Henry had to go down the slide and use the swing himself, before they got the idea. Yayra, the oldest, was the first to discover the steering wheels we had set up. "Wow! Look at this!" she exclaimed, turning one of the wheels. Then, of course, the boys all joined in.

Then, in 2004, a separate girls' home was constructed on the property. The government really wanted boys and girls to be separated, but they had given us permission to house them in separate rooms temporarily, with a promise that we would separate them as soon as possible.

In 2008, a 40 x 80 ft. pole barn type building was put up, covered but largely open-sided, to serve as an Activity Center. The building was purchased from FBI buildings in the U.S., and shipped, dismantled, in a sea container. John led Dave Riley, John Jones, Tom Harmon, and Joe Roberts to help set it up.

A garage, a couple of storage sheds, and a small staff apartment were added along the way, too, and finally a two-story middle school. Each new facility meant we could take in more children, or to do a better job of meeting the children's needs.

The construction of the middle school brought many challenges. We had planned it as a two-story building, to conserve space on our 8-acre allotment. We had also, of course, created all the financial estimates based on that. But Ghana had experienced an earthquake some years before, and as a result, had changed all their building regulations, especially for two-story buildings. We had to put in many more pillars than we had planned on, and those all contained expensive reinforcing rod. We began work, but quickly ran out of funds. As we sought new funding, time went by and prices increased greatly again.

Finally, in 2012, we started using the bottom portion for classes, even while workers continued to construct the second story. None of the rooms were plastered or painted, there were no chalkboards, and neither electricity nor bathrooms had been installed, but we desperately needed the classroom space, so we began to use what the Lord had already given us.

Then, in 2013, through a partnership with an organization called Girls for Africa, the last work was completed on the second story, the classrooms were finished, teachers' computers and projectors were installed, and we opened the school.

Another big challenge—the security fence

Another of the most difficult projects was building a protective cement block security fence around the whole property. Not only was it a big area to confine in such a way, but it was also difficult to fund. We talked to so many people asking them to help. The response was nearly always the same. Yes, they agreed that the fence was a needed project. Yes, they understood that thieves had already come and stolen some items, at the same time damaging the tractor. Yes, they understood that some of the children had just walked away, and that they needed this protection. Yes, they understood that the constant flow of outsiders across the property put the children at risk of kidnappers and child traffickers. But no, they didn't feel God was calling them to help with the project.

Why was God telling us to build the security fence, but not telling anyone to help with it? It was majorly discouraging. Were we confusing our own desires with God's will?

We still felt the fence was needed, so finally, we decided to start with the project one baby step at a time as we were able. The workers made cement posts and we put them in the end of the property closest to most of the buildings. That would not stop thieves, but it would serve as notice that this was private property. Later, we added more posts, until the property was surrounded by them at 8 ft. intervals. Later still, we added three rows of barbed wire between the posts. This still would not stop intruders, nor would it stop any determined child from wandering off in a moment of anger or discouragement. But for the most part, people did respect the barbed wire, and took new paths to their gardens or wherever. It greatly improved control of who was on the property.

The final step was to begin a firm cement barrier in between the posts. Again, we worked little by little until the property was finally protected. In late 2009, missionary Jim Driscoll put up a metal gate and a small guard house to complete the project. We all praised God that the seemingly impossible had again been accomplished by His grace.

Even better security—the dogs

Even better security was achieved when missionary Jim Driscoll brought the first dog to the home. These dogs had been specially bred to serve as guard dogs. They were large, so that both their appearance and their gruff bark intimidated would-be intruders. My husband John loves to tell the story of the group of thieves who put a ladder up to the barrier, intending to climb over and rob the home. The first of them got to the top, where they faced Zach, Jim's largest male dog. He growled seriously at the first site of them, and they backed out of there as fast as they could, scrambling over one another to see who could land in the get-away car first.

The female dog, Zoe, was smaller, but still very large. She would follow anyone on the other side of the barrier with her bark, so that we could always tell not only if someone was there, but also exactly where they were, and whether they were moving or standing still.

The dogs did not have to scare off too many intruders, though, for the word went out that there were big, ferocious dogs at Haven of Hope, and would-be thieves realized that the home would not be an easy target. On the other hand, the dogs were gentle with the children and quickly learned to know every person that should be there, easily distinguishing them from those who shouldn't be there.

Missionary help at Haven of Hope

We had begun Haven of Hope with only Ghanaian help and supervision, and us advising from far away by email, which was at that time unreliable because it could not be received directly at the home. We felt the project would be strengthened by missionaries living there. The first missionaries were Jim and Carolyn Driscoll, and Jere and Ruthann Gowin. Each added their own strengths.

Jim was good at making things and generally overseeing construction. He was also a good Bible teacher and a caring counselor, especially to the boys. Carolyn was a loving helper and charming hostess.

Jere was physically strong and agile, and helped the children learn tumbling. When he told a Bible story, the children's attention was riveted on him. He also had experience in Christian education. Ruthann connected well with many of the older girls. After a while, the Gowins moved to a ministry in northern Ghana with their own church group.

Doug and Sally Wayner later served. Doug was a graphic designer and used those skills on behalf of the home. He helped with sports and in many other areas. Sally contributed greatly by helping develop a special needs classroom for the school and training teachers for that ministry.

Haven of Hope had a natural attraction for missionaries, especially those who loved children. Several teachers and others gave nine months to two years' service. Laura Gillaspie was the first of those. She helped hone the mission statement for the school and helped teach the younger children.

Hannah Howard (Dillon) gave a special service of love. She had been helping in many ways including children's activities and leading Bible studies. One of the boys, I'll call him "Charlie," had to leave the home because his AIDS had become so advanced that not only might he be a danger to the other children, but even more so they might be a danger to him. His immune system had shut down so completely that any disease he caught might be fatal. "Charlie" went to his home village to be cared for by relatives for awhile, but as his disease progressed, it became untenable for them to care for him. We agreed to let "Charlie" come back to Haven of Hope and spend his last days in one of our apartments, away from the other children. Hannah graciously agreed to provide personal care. How lovingly she cared for "Charlie," putting his needs above her own, until the Lord took his wasted body home.

Short term teams

All who stayed longer made a lasting impact and created deep friendships with the children and staff. A constant flow of short-term teams, usually staying about two weeks, also made great contributions to the home, the school, and the lives of the children.[xxvii]

Spiritual growth

Some of the children came to Haven of Hope having learned of Christ and received Him in the street ministry. Others came to salvation through the constant efforts of our staff, American and Ghanaian, working together. Pastor Sammy Arthur personally led many children to salvation, as did missionary Jim Driscoll, Jere Gowin, and many others.

The staff found it worked best to hold Sunday worship at the home, particularly after the Activity Center was constructed. However, some Sundays the children visited other nearby churches.

When the first group of children were ready to show their faith in baptism, we arranged with Pastor Moses from the House of Deliverance Ministries to give them final instruction and examination, and to baptize them. He used a nearby river for the service. Later missionaries Doug and Sally Wayner prepared another group of children, and built a baptismal tank for use at the home.

One of our greatest joys was seeing some of the children spontaneously volunteer to evangelize in villages surrounding the home. We heard reports that some of them were very good and zealous teachers and caring personal evangelists.

Also greatly encouraging us concerning the children's spiritual development was the Bible Reading Club. We're not sure who was the leader in it, but it was the children's own idea. A group of them gathered each Saturday and began reading the Bible through, from cover to cover, as a group. One child would read while the others followed along in their Bibles, then another, and then another. I had the privilege of attending one of these Saturday Bible readings, and I was amazed at the rapt attention with which the children all followed. Of course, the club was voluntary, but a good many children attended and achieved their goal of reading the complete Bible.

Oh, the skills they learned!

Reading
Since most of the children had been living on the street, none of them knew how to read much if at

all when they arrived. Those skills were taught bit by bit, patiently, first by the mothers and later by teachers. They were also helped along greatly because virtually every team that visited the home read stories to the children. The children loved it, and they quickly learned to value reading. They learned that both new knowledge and enjoyable adventures were to be found in books. This made them work even harder.

Some of the teams also taught various phonics and other reading skills. It also helped that volunteers brought books on many subjects that appealed to both boys and girls, and to different ages. Soon Haven of Hope developed the finest library I have seen in Ghana or anywhere in Africa. It was heartening to me to see children reading books for themselves in their dorms and on the playground.

Writing

The schools in many African countries do not emphasize composition. Children learn to copy and recite. Largely through the motivation to write to their sponsors and encouraged by receiving letters in return, many of the Haven of Hope kids became excellent writers.

Gardening

It was always our desire to use the land God had provided for us to provide to the fullest extent possible for the nutritional needs of the children. While I admit we have never achieved this to the degree we desired, at least these city children received an introduction to the idea that they could raise food to improve their diets.

Pastor Sammy was specially good at leading the children to develop gardens. We also planted avocado and orange trees from seed, and they grew and produced fruit that the children enjoyed. Since we did not live permanently at Haven of Hope, the extent of the gardening depended on the experience and vision of the leaders at any given time. We are thankful for the start that was made, and we want to do all we can to encourage further agricultural experimentation.

Animal husbandry

Bernard Fianku, who worked with ECM's street ministry, started an animal husbandry project raising goats. Since goat is the children's favorite meat, this was a very popular project, and the children were eager to learn to care for the goats so that they would reproduce well.

After missionary Jim Driscoll purchased the first male and female guard dogs, he began to breed dogs. The food was expensive for these large dogs, and there were veterinary and other expenses, but the pups sold at a good profit. Several of the boys became involved in the care of the dogs. Not only was it good for them to learn about the dogs' needs, but it was a natural way for them to learn about breeding, pregnancy, birth, nursing, etc.

Sports & physical activities

Through the varied interests of the many visiting teams, the children received an introduction to a wide range of sports and physical activities. However, their favorites have always been soccer (called football in Ghana) and choreographed dancing. Mostly boys played soccer, but sometimes girls joined in, too. The Haven of Hope team played matches with local schools and with a nearby orphanage, Rafiki. Both genders enjoyed the dancing. The children put on admirable exhibitions of their dancing talents at parents' programs for the school, and sometimes danced to choreographed worship songs at local churches.

Welding

A member of the Girls for Africa team taught some of the children welding skills. We were glad to see both boys and some girls voluntarily join in. Practical skills!

Arts & Crafts

Many individuals and teams taught the children a variety of arts and crafts skills. Two that became quite substantially developed were jewelry making and sewing. Some of the girls learned to make beautiful clothes for themselves and others before they finished high school. In all the children, a spirit of creativity was cultivated that was very beautiful to see. One of the girls went on to study fashion design in university.

Household skills

At one point, we and the Ghanaian staff realized that with cooks and cleaners and others serving at the home, children could easily become accustomed to being served by others. Together, we decided to make a deliberate effort to cultivate an independent spirit as far as meeting one's own needs was concerned, as well as a willingness to serve others. We also wanted to make sure that children at Haven of Hope learned the basic skills culturally appropriate to their gender, so that they would be able to function without hindrance in adult life.

When the old-style wringer washing machines broke down, they were not replaced, and children became responsible to wash their own clothing and bedding by hand, just as they would do if they lived in a "real" family setting. Children were assigned small, individual garden plots to plant, maintain, and harvest for the good of all. Cleaning assignments were rotated, and girls were assigned to help the cooks prepare meals so that they learned how to make Ghanaian dishes.

More challenges—tough children

Most of the children thrived and were happy and contented at Haven of Hope. However, there were some challenging children. One of these I will call "Mimi." She ran away several times before we could secure the property with a fence. Sometimes she just refused to cooperate with the mothers. But her most difficult habit was her screaming. If things did not go her way, she would just scream. She was not screaming words—just aaah! Screaming. Nothing the mothers tried would stop it, and it could go on for 45 minutes at times. It was wearing on the mothers and disturbing to the other children. Several times we almost expelled "Mimi," but there was no other place for her to go than back to the streets.

In time, "Mimi's" screaming slowly subsided and she began to open up and show interest in life. She had long revolted against attempts to teach her, saying, "as for me, I will not learn."

Finally, after coming to Christ in her early teens, "Mimi" decided she wanted to learn. Sadly, she was so far behind that it was no longer feasible to help her catch up. I tried tutoring her in math during one of my visits and found her at about the beginning third grade level. She could not pass the required exams to go on in school, so we recommended vocational training. "Mimi" attended culinary school and did very well there. On one of my visits to Ghana, she led some of the other girls in preparing a fancy bread for me. Delicious. "Mimi" glowed with pride, and I was so proud of her.

"Stoner" was our most challenging boy. He showed a real talent for art, but he like to imagine himself a tough dude, and was often in trouble for fighting, stealing, etc. We were all sitting in worship one Sunday when in a split second "Stoner" jumped up and began tussling on the floor angrily with another boy.

When counseled, "Stoner" would seem to be contrite, only to repeat his offenses again and again. He became rude to the mothers and we finally decided we had to release him to family members, even though we knew his situation was very difficult. "Stoner" continues to flirt with his desire to be a worldly tough dude, but we are sure he has heard the Gospel and knows that Word of God provides the only sure and firm foundation for life.

Pastor Sammy with the younger children during the school worship time

More challenges—official disfavor for children's homes

Another of our challenges at Haven of Hope came from Ghanaian government sources, but ultimately from the United Nations. It was an official disfavor towards orphanages and children's homes,[xxviii] based on studies that showed children do better in family situations. (Duh!)

Of course, all of us at Every Child Ministries agree that children do better in families, preferably families with a loving father and mother. If that were an option for any of the Haven of Hope children, we would have returned them to their families in the blink of an eye. However, we found these children alone on the street, wandering in and out of heavy downtown traffic, and entirely without adult supervision. For various reasons, returning them to their families was not feasible. That's why we decided to do our best to become a substitute family for them, so that at least they would know that somebody in this world cared about them. We also wanted to become for them a Christian family where they learned about a loving Father and Creator in an atmosphere of acceptance.

This all came to a head when we received a group called KaeMe. Volunteers from the U.S., mostly college students, were guided by a Ghanaian from the Department of Social Welfare to compile information about children's homes in the country, and to advise and inform us of Ghana's official position that children's homes and orphanages should be discouraged.

They interviewed the children privately one by one, and they were not happy that the children liked it there and considered Haven of Hope their "home." Their home, we were informed, was with their parents, and a children's home could never be their home. They made it clear that we were to work to turn around the children's thinking, and to work towards reconciling them to their families. Ghana was working, they said, towards closing children's homes. All children would be better off, they insisted, with their parents or other relatives, no matter what the situation, even if it meant the children would be returned to the streets.

This was quite a shock to us, since we thought we were doing a good thing for the children. We began to make some initial steps toward conforming to their guidelines, and for a while, called the whole place Haven of Hope Academy and boarding school, de-emphasizing the children's home part.

However, we noticed that despite all that KaeMe had told us, Ghana Social Welfare continued to ask us to receive children from various difficult circumstances, including one whose father was trying to kill him.

After we had stepped out of our roles as International Directors and moved back to the role of missionaries, the director who succeeded us decided to stop the move toward calling it a boarding school (although that was a part of the program). It was decided go back to calling it a children's home. By that time, some officials had explained that Ghana needs some children's homes, and they only intended to close those who were not meeting the needs of the children. So, we are relieved for now, but we realize that the future of Haven of Hope depends on the outlook and decisions of officials within the country, and since the United Nations is a major funding agency for Ghana, it also depends on the views currently in vogue there.

As for us, we're all about encouraging families to stay together whenever feasible and safe for the children, but looking at the brokenness of this world, we're also highly in favor of keeping all options open when it comes to helping vulnerable children—as long as those options don't cross Biblical injunctions, of course.

After Ninth Grade—

We had originally thought of creating both a high school and a vocational school. However, Ghanaian high schools are highly specialized, meaning just one school would not suffice, and vocational training opportunities were available elsewhere. Therefore, the decision was eventually made to end the training at Haven of Hope after Middle School (ninth grade), but to continue support and a certain amount of supervision through higher levels of education, as long as their sponsors were willing and able to continue. Virtually all Ghanaian high schools have a boarding section, which could provide a place for the high school students to live, and they could return to Haven of Hope during holidays.

At this writing, almost all the original children were either returned to relatives or are now in high school or university. Several have completed university and have found jobs. Their experience at Haven of Hope seems to have prepared them well, and we are thankful.

Several of them have befriended us on Facebook and often write to express appreciation and love. One, hearing that I had undergone an operation, wrote, "I wish it was me paying your hospital bills."

Did it make a difference?

As we evaluate our experiences at Haven of Hope, two things are clear: It was certainly the most expensive venture ECM has ever undertaken, but it is also the venture that has had the deepest influence on the lives of the children in that ministry. Even when I consider those who would not be selected as "success stories," I see that Haven of Hope had a very positive and long-lasting effect on their lives. It will be exciting to see what God does through them in the future.

5. Seeing Slave Children Initiative vs. Shrine Slavery, Ghana (1999)

I became aware of shrine slavery on our first exploratory trip to Ghana. It happened just about the time that I was realizing that Sunday schools were not going to be an effective method to reach children in Ghana as they were in Congo. I was pondering these thoughts even as I was teaching a training seminar for Sunday school teachers along with John and Alan Cox, who then served as president of ECM's board.

During a break time, a man came up to us and handed us each a t-shirt saying something like, "Stop Trokosi Now." When I asked what trokosi was, he replied, "It is a form of slavery we have here in my country." I was shocked. I thought slavery was an evil that was long gone from the earth. The man said he was Stephen Awudi Gadry of Trokosi Abolition Fellowship. He said there were places in Ghana called "traditional or fetish shrines" where idol gods were worshipped. The priests of some of these shrines took slaves, often young girls, and used them for sexual purposes as well as for work.

We didn't have time to talk much more about it, but my head was reeling. Could this be true? If so, it definitely had to be a horrifically negative influence on the children of Ghana.

Checking it out

After I returned home, I kept thinking about what Stephen had told me. Could this be true? I checked it out on the internet, and found that it was true, and that much had been written about it. The organization that had the biggest web presence on the issue was International Needs (IN). I began corresponding with their Ghanaian leaders, asked many questions, and arranged for them to guide me on a visit to Ghana the following year. Besides getting a legal presence for ECM set up in Ghana, one of my primary goals was to check out the practice of trokosi and see it for myself.

Seeing it for myself

International Needs arranged for one of their field workers named Wisdom Mensah to drive me to the appropriate locations in the Volta Region. I visited a priest who had liberated his trokosi slaves and a training center where IN gave vocational training to the women after liberation. The most moving and profound experience of the day was a visit to a former trokosi. I'll call her

"Fanny." Fanny was a sad-looking woman then in her thirties.

Fanny's story

She told me that at the age of thirteen, her parents had told her they were going on a trip. As they walked along the path, she realized that they were not going to the destination her parents had mentioned.

After a while, they arrived at a traditional shrine. She remained outside while her parents went in to talk with the priest. She overheard enough of their conversation to realize to her horror that she was going to be left at the shrine.

Her parents left by another way, not even saying goodbye. The priest called her in and ordered her to strip. Fanny had to obey, standing there naked, ashamed, and terrified before the priest, who seemed to her like a very old man.

She learned that she had just become a trokosi, but it was years later before she learned why. Her initiation involved having sex with the old priest, being bathed with some herbs mixed in water, and being paraded naked around the shrine. Fanny only wanted to die.

As a trokosi, she was considered a "wife of the gods." She didn't know that educated supporters of traditional religion were saying she was a queen, and that it was a privilege for her to have sex with the priest, since his genitals had been dedicated to the gods. She only knew that she had to work hard every day in the priest's fields, dust the repulsive-looking idols with some kind of powder, and endure the priest's sexual advances when it was her turn. She never experienced affection from the priest, nor any friendship from the other trokosi, about 30 in the shrine. She never enjoyed a good meal, being forced to survive on scraps of garbage. It was strictly forbidden her to eat even a morsel of the produce from the priest's gardens. Hunger and pain were her constant companions.

"Did you ever just tell the priest 'no', when he wanted sex ? " I asked.

"Oh, yes," Fanny replied. "All of us told him that at one time or another. When we told him 'no', we were given two choices. It was the only time we had a choice about anything. He would lay two things on the ground in front of us. One was a whip, and the other was a bunch of broken bottles. We could take a whipping, and if we chose that, shrine elders held us down. It was long and hard.

Or, we could kneel on the broken bottles, holding both arms up in the air for hours."

The saddest part of Fanny's story was that the only person who would give her food to alleviate her constant hunger in those days was a Muslim man. It was a Christian organization that liberated her, but she was so grateful to the Muslim man, that when he offered to marry her, she felt she could not refuse. Fanny was a believer, but her new husband refused to let her go to church or openly practice her faith in any way. As we talked, his son kept looking in the window, watching us carefully.

A seesaw of misery

When I returned to my room that night, Fanny's story gnawed at my heart. I felt as if I had just lifted the lid off hell itself and peeked in. To think there were still many other girls bound in this horrific form of slavery! Fanny had been sucked into that system at the tender age of 13. I thought back to when I was 13, possibly the most painful and lonely time of my life. I could almost physically feel her pain.

I knew ECM had to help, and I had to lead the charge. I could not just pretend I knew nothing about this. I could not ignore it. I had learned, though, that it costs about $200 to liberate one girl and her children. (I had learned that trokosi end up with an average of three children through regular rape by the priest.) There were hundreds of trokosi, so it would cost many thousands of dollars to help them.

My mind reeled back and forth. We HAD to help the trokosi. We COULD NOT possibly help them. We were already struggling to keep up with the projects we'd committed to. Then Fanny's sad face would flash into my mind, and I knew we had to help. But there was no way. We totally lacked the means to do anything. But we just had to. Back and forth I went.

One thought brings breakthrough!

Finally, the Lord brought this thought to mind: "Don't I know lots of people who would gladly give a one-time gift of $200 to free one slave girl?"

Yes, of course. When I began to look at it in individual terms rather than in the cost of the whole project, it seemed much more feasible. I prayed committing the issue to the Lord and determined to recommend to the Board that ECM take this on as a project.

It's a go! ECM goes abolitionist.

When I reported to the Board on the trip, they also sensed the pain of the girls trapped in that system. They readily and unanimously gave their approval for ECM to get involved, all of us knowing the enormity of that step.

I began to correspond with International Needs about partnering in the project. It was a long process involving an official, written agreement which was the result of much discussion and some compromise.[xxix]

IN was leading the negotiations with three shrines. ECM provided substantial funding, prayer, and publicity as we learned from IN one of the methods by which liberation was being achieved for shrine slaves. It took a lot longer than we expected or wanted, and we learned that in such negotiations, there are many turns and twists, and no guaranteed outcome.

Advocacy

I began speaking everywhere I could about the practice of trokosi and writing about it through all channels available. As God had shown me on my first visit, when faced with the awful reality of this practice, many people wanted to help. Some reached deep into their budget to give the $200 that we estimated would be needed to free one slave girl.

Fanny's story was especially effective, and I never tired of telling it, or failed to feel her pain all over again. Even today I can barely think of it without tears coming to my eyes. By faith, we had promised IN $25,000 to help with the liberation. We achieved our goal, sending the funds in three installments.

First Liberation at last!—Three shrines of the Agave area

Finally, we received word that all three shrines had agreed to free their trokosi. A date for liberation was set. Excitedly, I purchased my airline ticket to go and witness the event for which we had worked and prayed so hard.

Arriving early at the set location, I prayed over the ground soon to be hallowed by the liberation of slaves who, through no fault of their own, had been bound to wicked spirits of idols. They had been "atoned" to pay for the sins of the family through perpetual slavery and suffering.

Now they would soon be free to learn of Jesus, who had already given Himself to atone for their sins and those of their family—those of us all. I could easily anticipate what that was going to mean to these poor girls who had no hope of ever being freed. I was nearly overcome with emotion and anticipation.

I was asked to give a speech at that program. It did not bother me that nearly a thousand people were watching. I felt a deep need to do all I could to celebrate that momentous occasion.

As part of the agreement with the shrine, no more trokosi were ever to be taken into that place. The practice of slavery was to be forever ended there. Another part of the agreement promised that the girls liberated would receive an opportunity for vocational training in one of several programs of their choice.

At the end of the liberation day, I was nearing exhaustion. My face had turned beat red in the heat. I was too tired to eat or bathe. Back at my hotel room, I just lay on my bed and tried to process all I had seen and experienced that day. I did not get up until the next morning.

2nd Liberation— Aklidokpo Shrine

After our first liberation with International Needs, it was obvious that the relationship IN desired with us was more as donors and less as partners. Considering this, our staff decided they were ready to try to liberate the slaves under ECM's auspices.

We received word about a shrine called Aklidokpo at Adidome, a town in the N Tongu District of the

Volta Region. Pastor Mark Wisdom of Fetish Slaves Liberation Movement (FESLIM) said his group had started a liberation there but had run out of funds along the way and was unable to complete the work. We agreed to join FESLIM in a partnership liberation.

That liberation took place on January 22, 2004. I went with the negotiating team the day before the event as they reviewed the agreement with the shrine owner and priest. There was ready agreement. The shrine owner said that they inherited these idols from their ancestors and they had always been a source of trouble to them. The liberation was to them a godsend.

Ed White of Great Commission Resources, one of our funding partners in the project, traveled to Ghana to experience the liberation and record the stories of some of the women.

Girls from a local school had prepared a traditional dance for the occasion. "How appropriate!" I thought. They *should* rejoice. When shrine slavery is ended here, the school will no longer be losing its female students to this wicked practice."

3rd Liberation—Sovigbenor Shrine

After that liberation, ECM faced the question of whether we would liberate only trokosi, those intended to atone for the sins of the family, or whether we would include other forms of shrine slavery as well. Many forms of shrine slavery were abundant in the Volta Region and into Togo and Benin. Many carried the names of the gods to which they were devoted or sacrificed. One of the most common was "Yevesi." These were slaves of the thunder god, Yeve. Our worker Judith had been a Yevesi, and she felt strongly that Yevesi needed to be liberated, too.

That led us to the Sovigbenor Shrine in Aflao, a border city with road entrance to Togo on the southeastern most part of Ghana. Things were going well until a newspaper reporter became interested and put an article in a local newspaper in Ghana. That led to pressure on the shrine from those who support traditional fetish worship. The leading group seeking to support traditional worship of the gods was (and is) the Afrikania Mission. Because it has the word "mission" in its name, some assume it to be a Christian group. It is just the opposite; it is anti-Christian in practice. This is virtually the only group that approves and promotes the practice of shrine slavery.[xxx]

Finally, the shrine agreed to liberate its Yevesi and ECM agreed not to put it on TV or put it out on the news. It was announced only to our own following and to those of the local community who attended the liberation. The event was held December 9, 2007, in the yard outside another shrine on one of the long strips of land in the area's many lagoons.

Since these Yevesi had not recently been confined to the shrine, but had been given "flaxaxo," or permission to live outside the shrine but still tightly under the shrine's control, they had developed small businesses. In place of vocational training, ECM made a financial contribution to enable the women to strengthen those businesses. Some grew pepper, dried it and stored it until the off-season when prices were highest before selling it.

One of the Yevesi freed in that event happened to be one of two wives of the head priest of Yeve in the area. We did not realize who they were when our staff began to visit her and her husband. However, it was evident that both were immediately interested in the Gospel.

After the staff paid numerous visits to the home, I heard that the priest had professed faith in Christ. I'll call him Dabu. Now he faced a great crisis. What was to become of his priesthood, and the idols under his care?[xxxi]

After some time, we heard that Dabu wanted to liberate his 53 shrine slaves, Yevesi, servants of the thunder god. Unlike the priests in the other shrines, he did not request payment in return for the liberation. He only asked transport money, "to tell the priests serving under him" of his decision, he said.

I attended the liberation ceremony held in the enclosure of a home near the home of the priest. We gave each woman a new piece of cloth and a financial gift to enable them to strengthen their little businesses.

Initially, Dabu planned to arrange for bandits to come in the night and destroy the shrine idols. However, some advised him that this could cause trouble, since the idols belonged to the whole family, and not just him. Next, he planned to tell the family that he was done with the idols, so if anyone wanted them, they should come and get them or take over responsibility for them.

Dabu seemed to do well for awhile. We gave him a player with the New Testament recorded on it, and he played it over and over, even receiving many from the immediate community into his yard to listen.

He visited church a time or two, but never seemed to get connected. It was hard for us to tell whether he felt welcome at church or not. There is much fear of priests even in the Christian community, and Dabu may have felt that. He never made Christian fellowship a regular part of his life. Was his conversion real? We believed it was. Now, I just have to leave it in God's hands. The Scripture says He knows those who are His (2 Timothy 2:19).

I worked hard at the project, which I called "Initiative against Shrine Slavery." I wrote much on the internet, providing the first Wikipedia article on the subject. I was pleased that what I wrote was copied and recopied to other sites. Hopefully it influenced public opinion. That was my aim in writing.

With some of my Ghanaian co-workers in the initiative against shrine slavery

I also spoke on the topic at every opportunity, seeking to raise public opinion against the practice, and seeking to raise funds to continue fighting it.

ECM worked hard at giving those who were liberated opportunities to make their own way in life, with God's help. Sharon Aldrich held two seminars in which she taught the women to sew colorful cloth bags for sale, and sewing machines were given to some of the women. Several people taught them to string beads. Both the staff and several teams helped in discipling the women.

Most former shrine slaves have never known love or acceptance, so it's very important to me to show them the love of Jesus every chance I can.

It was hard going all the way. The first missionary we sent to help, Micky Beaujean, developed health issues and returned home. However, she donated all the funds she had raised to the project, and they were used to buy property just outside Aflao, which became the "New Life Center."

The second missionary, Hannah Howard, served with the Sogakope workers for a year and led a very old woman to Christ. She had first told Hannah and her helper that it was too late for her, since she was "already given to the devil." Eventually, Hannah decided the project needed a couple or family.

The third missionaries, James and Denise Forkkio, were a married couple, he a Ghanaian and she an American. One of the shrine slaves told them she had chosen to come to the shrine.[xxxii] They became disillusioned with the project, believing the women were not really slaves, at least in the kind they had accustomed to thinking of. Eventually they left ECM. Happily, they went to serve with another mission in another part of the world. Years later, they called and apologized for the way they had judged us so harshly. We greatly appreciated that, and our friendship was restored. They eventually started another ministry to Ghana, focused on helping the poor.

The final missionary, Cassandra Williams, was an African-American who went to serve with the Aflao team with very little personal support. She made several significant contributions to the project, but she ended up disillusioned with the staff and they with her. She returned to the U.S.

and continues serving today with another ministry.

I had always felt the project would greatly benefit from missionary support and supervision, but getting and keeping missionaries for it was like pulling demons out of hell (NOT to imply that our missionaries were demons). It was high-powered spiritual warfare, and through our lack of faith or sufficient prayer or God's will or whatever, we had only limited success.

One of our staff members, Judith, had the advantage of having been both a trokosi and a Yevesi, so she had much inside insight and experience. The grandmother of another staff member, Mary, had been a trokosi, and remembers with deep sadness and horror the undignified way in which her grandmother's corpse was treated after death. She, too, had personal insight into the system.

However, one of the problems we consistently faced with many of our staff in Ghana was what seemed to us their grandiose expectations of what we could do for them financially, and this was true even of some of our best workers. I attribute this problem to two root causes: One was Ghana's declared intention to become a middle-class country. Although much poverty persisted, most of our staff we would consider at least on the fringes of lower-middle class to middle class. Certainly they were not even close to abject poverty, but they all felt poor. Our modest and frugal ways worked better in desperately poor countries like Congo.

The second and perhaps more influential root cause I believe was the widespread saturation of so many Ghanaian churches with "healthy-wealthy" teachings. Most Ghanaians expected that as God's children they should have first-class everything, and that their employer should furnish that for them. All our workers had readily agreed to their salaries, and they were paid fully, consistently and on time. But ECM's best was often seen as an insult to them. They tended to feel they were being cheated because they really "should" be paid a lot more. This affected all our projects, but particularly the initiative against shrine slavery. It was also responsible for the disillusionment of many of our missionaries with some of the Ghanaian staff. For me personally, it was a source of endless frustration and sorrow.

The slave project seemed to do great things for awhile, but after four liberations, we hit a time when all our efforts seemed to yield small results if any.

At that time, the staff mentioned that one of the CHRAJ (Commission on Human Rights and Administrative Justice) officers knew of some trokosi who were seeking to be freed. We met the women, began to help them, and began to gather their stories. After we had already committed to a liberation, we discovered that some of them had been out of the shrine for some years. We went through with a small liberation ceremony acknowledging that they were officially free from the shrine, but it was not the kind of life-altering liberation we were seeking.

However, we discovered that these women had actually freed themselves as a result of the evangelistic and discipling ministry of a local church. We were greatly encouraged by this, since we had always been told that trokosi could not be freed except through the direct intervention of an outside group. Since it appeared that all of the shrines that were ready to liberate had done so, we decided to end our liberation efforts and concentrate on saturating the area with evangelistic and discipling efforts. Our hope is that as this is done, the strongholds of the shrines will eventually be cast down and those held in spiritual bondage liberated by the power of the Gospel.

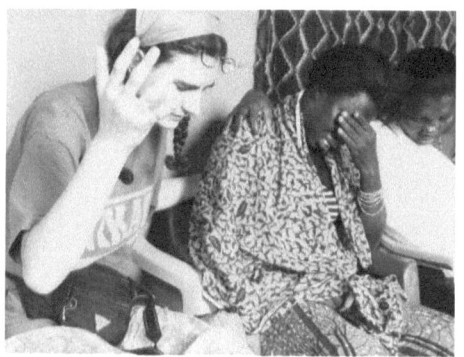

Marissa prays with one of the former shrine slaves

In the process, one of the highlights of the project was when one of our granddaughters, Marissa, oldest child of our oldest daughter Carrie and her husband Bill Boehmer, visited the project. A strong prayer warrior with a deep love for God, Marissa was thrilled to join in prayer for some of the women who had been liberated.

Ritual slavery is tied to idol worship (called fetish worship in Ghana), which was a part of African Traditional Religion. We realized that as churches were strengthened with biblical doctrine and began to reach the children of their communities, and as adherents of the various traditional shrines were evangelized, the bonds of slavery would be loosened until it would have no more power over the people.

Togo and Benin

To this end, we did Sunday school seminars in many villages of the Volta Region of Ghana and in Togo and Benin as well. As we came into Togo on the first trip, I recognized a traditional shrine along the road. We stopped and asked questions about it. We learned that the main part of the shrine was on a small island we could see from where we were. It could be reached only by boat. On the outside shrine wall was an intriguing painting. It had a picture of a snake standing up as I had seen some do when they were ready to attack. It had a large, flattened head, and on its head was painted a little baby. I asked what it meant and was told that people often came to the shrine seeking the ability to conceive. The picture showed their snake god, which they called Dhan, as the giver of children.

Another year, as our team entered Benin, we saw shrines to Dhan in Cotonou. We were told real snakes were kept in those shrines. I didn't go anywhere near them to check it out!

While in those countries, I visited several historic and cultural sites about which I had read. We also targeted key areas for ministry where we felt that key historic events would likely have impacted the spiritual climate of the area. One year I did a

Sunday school seminar in Notsie, a Togo town of historic consequence to the Ewe tribe. They had once been imprisoned by a certain king, had broken out, and had migrated into what later became the Volta Region of Ghana. My Ghanaian coworker Evelyn and I slept in a hotel next to the remains of that ancient prison. We needed local elders to guide our visit to the site, so we listened to their history and presented them with tracts from World Missionary Press, which they received gladly. Then one of the elders took us to the site and explained more of their history. We stepped around several small shrines where blood sacrifices were offered.

That night my dreams were invaded by faces of beautiful women with long flowing hair. Bodyless, they seemed to be floating in the air. They were smiling at me, but I instinctively knew they were evil. I awoke screaming and shuddering. Evelyn rushed to my bed, concerned. I explained the dream to her, and we prayed together, claiming God's protection over us and the seminar we were teaching, and refusing any attack of the enemy. I went back to sleep and slept well.

I had read the accounts of human sacrifice taking place by the hundreds in in the 1800's in Abomey, capital of what was then Dahomey (now modern Benin). Countless beheadings were done there when a new king was installed, and to renew annually the power of the sitting king. I was interested to visit this site and to better understand how it affected how shrine slavery as well as idol worship had been so persistent in this culture. Abomey was a sprawling city, for each succeeding king had built his "palace" (complex of mud structures) adjacent to the last one, and each family retained residence in their section of the old palaces. I was disappointed that inside the inner part of the old palaces, photography was not permitted, nor did they even offer postcard pictures for sale. I had to check my camera at the gate.

I knew that the common practice was the execution of all the wives of the king by burying them alive with him, ostensibly to serve him in the afterlife. At one site, the guide told us that here is where the wives of a certain king were buried with him because they loved him so much that they "volunteered" to die with him. I did not imagine that it was the kind of 'choice' in which they had anything to say about it.

When they came to one of the most sacred shrines, it was covered with a low-hanging thatch roof. We were free to go in, but I chose not to do so, remembering my experience in Notsie. I did note that dried bones littered the entire exterior around the building. At Abomey, too, we were able to leave a few Gospel tracts in the local language, as we had all along the way.

Along the way home from Abomey, we noticed walls that looked very old around parts of one village. Knowing that some ancient walls were purportedly made with mud mixed with human blood of conquered enemies, these walls sparked my interest. We stopped and I asked a few questions. Soon messengers sent for the elders of the village. We took advantage of the opportunity to listen to the history of their village, and they affirmed that the walls were made just as I had heard. At one point, I didn't take enough notes, and one of the elders scolded me. "This is important. Write this down," he said. I gladly complied. After listening to their history and seeing the sites of their traditional rituals, they asked me what I wanted to tell them. Yes! I was accompanied by a Togolese pastor, but it was very clear that they were interested in what I, the outsider, might have to say. I assured them that their history was very interesting to me. This seemed to please them. Hazel Hermosillo was with me, and I glanced at her, pleading with my eyes for prayer. Then very carefully and in considerable detail, I was able to share the Gospel with them. They all listened intently—the chief and his sons, the village priests and priestess, all their magic men and village elders. When I finished, I asked them what they thought of what I had shared. I find this open-ended question a good way to judge someone's response.

The chief answered. This is something new to them. This is very deep. They will have to give this some serious thought.

Fair enough. I assured them that Christ stands always ready to hear us when we turn to Him in faith and repentance. They invited us to come again. Sadly, I was never able to do so, but I asked the local pastors to try to follow up with the village.

In Ghana where ECM had its base, my Ghanaian co-worker Judith, a former trokosi slave herself, frequently accompanied me to visit shrines and present the Gospel to the adherents we found there, whether priests and priestesses, trokosi, or adherents in various other capacities. I could see that many of them were clearly interested, but were afraid to leave the shrine for cultural and family reasons. I knew the Holy Spirit could break through that. The shrine slaves themselves had been uniquely prepared to understand and appreciate the Gospel because they were forced to serve as living sacrifices in an attempt to atone for the sins of others, yet no matter how many generations of girls atoned, those sins could never be forgiven but had to continue to be atoned for until the end of time.

I discovered that even the priests and priestesses realized that though not officially shrine slaves, they too were spiritually enslaved by their gods. I felt that Traditional Religion was a thick wall, but one that had a lot of cracks in it. To my knowledge, Judith and I were one of the first to personally visit adherents of traditional religion and invite them to Christ. We did hear that a Baptist pastor named Mark Wisdom had also sought to share Christ with some of them some years earlier. There may have been others, but it certainly was not something that was common to do. Shrine adherents were typically and massively overlooked in evangelistic efforts, even though there were many churches in Ghana.

I understood that this work perhaps took a special calling. My understanding of all things occult and all things identified with idolatry was that as a Christian I must stay as far away from them as I could. Yet along the way as I worked with the slave project, I began to see the priests and priestesses not only as practitioners of a wicked system, but as people over whom my Savior wept. I had to do all I could to reach them, even if this meant contacting them at their shrines. One of the topics I found most effective in talking with them were the unusual events that occurred while Jesus was on the cross and at the moment He died. They had offered many sacrifices, yet they had never seen the sky turn dark at noonday, the earth tremble, or the curtain blocking the way to one of their shrines rip in two pieces by itself. They readily recognized that these were "God" events that verified Christ's ministry. I believe that many shrine adherents and even leaders do feel their need for a Savior, and I pray that they may yet yield their hearts to Him and come out of that wicked system.

6. Seeing trafficked children, Ghana & Uganda (2009)

Training as a Slavery Investigator

As I was seeking every possible way to fight shrine slavery, I heard of a week of intensive training being offered in San Francisco by the anti-slavery organization "Not for Sale." The title of the training intrigued me—"Slavery Investigator Academy." That was just what I aspired to become—a slavery investigator!

The training, taken in August 2009, was thorough and enlightening, covering many aspects of modern-day slavery and human trafficking, presented by experts involved in the fight. Despite some liberal bias shown by some presenters here and there, I learned a lot that was very useful. When I went in for my oral exam, I presented them a paper outlining the facts I knew about shrine slavery, one of the few kinds of slavery they had not mentioned.

I never heard from them any more about it. Maybe because it involved religion, they did not want to associate themselves with it. I added many cases of shrine slavery to "Slavery Map" online, before I decided to be thankful for what I had learned and go on, using my new knowledge in ECM's own work. The map was later taken down and the web address defaulted to the "Not For Sale" site.

From this training and from my own experiences working against ritual slavery, I developed training on child trafficking which I presented in several seminars to all the staff in Ghana and Uganda. I knew that anyone working with street kids and other marginalized children was bound to be exposed to many kinds of child trafficking. I wanted them to recognize it when they saw it, record sufficient significant details, and report it effectively. I hoped ECM might become involved in freeing some children from its ugly grasp, and in working to prevent it in as many cases as possible.

One of the key concepts I learned in my training with NFS was that in addition to helping victims of trafficking and slavery, other projects could aim at the prevention of these horrors.

Central Region, Ghana
My first opportunity to do something to prevent or at least slow down child trafficking came in Ghana. Our workers had long remarked that a very high percentage of street children came from

the Central Region, to the immediate west of Accra, the capital city. When I shared the highlights of my training with them, they again shared the conviction that the Central Region was a major source area for child trafficking. While I was there training staff in these matters, the news came out that the police had intercepted two busloads of children being trafficked out of the Central Region. For me, that cemented my resolve.

I knew that an active child sponsorship program would do a lot to decrease trafficking in the area. Sponsored children are almost never trafficked. It's not that sponsorship meets all the family's needs, but it offers enough hope that they become much less receptive to the traffickers' lies.

As we looked around the area, we did not find a place that seemed acceptable as a base of operations, so I developed a plan to use one of our annual Fall fundraising banquets to raise what would be needed to create such a base.

"Stop Child Trafficking at the Source" had strong appeal, and people responded generously. Construction of a modest center was begun in the town of Birwa. Soon after, staff identified some of the neediest children of the community and we began looking for child sponsors.

Today that program is still active, and none of those families have lost children to child trafficking. God later provided a missionary couple, Jim and Carolyn Driscoll, to work in the Birwa area. They have found many ways to help poor families so that the parents are better able to support their children, and the lure of child traffickers grows less.

Karamoja, Uganda

The second place a "Stop Child Trafficking at the Source" was begun was a group of districts in NE Uganda, known as Karamoja.

ECM had been working with street children in Kampala, the capital city. Most had turned out to be Karimojong children, sons and daughters of a proud pastoral people who were experts in all things related to cattle, but ill-adapted to city life. Children (and others) kept coming to the city because of drought, famine, and other extreme conditions in their own homeland-Karamoja.

ECM had placed 21 of these children in a boarding school through child sponsorship, and they were doing beautifully. We discovered that they were highly intelligent and very adaptable. We also learned that many of them had been trafficked to the city, where they were assigned a master whom they were to call "mother." The proceeds of their begging were not their own, but went through the "mother" to a master who owned all of them.

We began to see that the only long-term hope for these children was to do something to help them stay with their families in the homeland. This eventually led to a child sponsorship project there, today called the "Karamoja Homeland Hope Center."

7. Seeing War-affected children, N Uganda (2006)

I don't remember exactly when or how I began hearing about the problems children in northern Uganda were facing due to Joseph Kony and his "Lord's Resistance Army" (LRA). I do know that I heard about it over several years from multiple sources, and that each time I heard it, my heart was wrenched within me for the poor children torn from their families at gunpoint, usually at night, even as they were sleeping right next to their parents.

The only hope for these children to survive was to become soldiers in Kony's army. Their initiation was to kill their own parents, and they were forced to clap as they witnessed others do the same. How could these children live normal lives thereafter, even if they somehow escaped servitude with the LRA? The phenomenon of "night commuters," children from village and rural settings who traveled by foot to the cities to find some semblance of 'protection', made sense only in light of the atrocities they would witness, or worse, be forced to participate in, if they stayed home.

Every time I read a new article or heard a new broadcast about the insane lifestyle being forced on families in northern Uganda, I prayed for the children there. I prayed for God's hand of protection upon them, for God's mercy and healing in their lives, and strength and wisdom for all who were seeking to help them. I learned that many businesses and public places like banks had opened their doors at night to welcome children who filled the floor laid out like logs as they slept. I heard of shelters being opened for them, and every available place being filled with children seeking to escape the wrath of the LRA.

I learned that Kony was a combination of a rebel fighter having some vague discontent with the national government, and occult leader. Like many occult groups, he used the Lord's name, while his deeds contradicted everything the Lord taught. He was hard to figure out. His stated goal was to reinstate the observance of the Ten Commandments as law, yet he and his followers murdered freely and forced young children to do the same.

When I hear about children under such oppression, a permanent weight and sadness comes over my soul. I felt that weight for the children of northern Uganda. As I prayed for them, I only yearned more and more to help them somehow. Surely since Every Child Ministries was for "the forgotten children of Africa," as the

tagline I'd chosen for ECM stated, these poor children must be included.
But what to do, and how?

In spite of this strong desire to help, I kept giving myself three reasons why this was not feasible. First, without even asking him, I already "knew" my husband would never agree to getting involved in another major project. I had too many "irons in the fire" already, as my dad used to say.

Second, I "knew" the board of Every Child Ministries would never agree, and for the same reason. We were struggling to meet the needs of all our other projects already. How could we think of adding one more? My intuition predicted the Board would not even consider it.

Finally, I knew there were other missions working in the area. I told myself we would only be stepping on someone else's feet if ECM was to enter this field.

Then, in just one week, the Lord knocked down every one of my excuses.[xxxiii] One day I received an unexpected and unsolicited letter from Action International, another mission agency working in northern Uganda. Their director said that they, and as he saw it, every other mission agency working in northern Uganda, was overwhelmed with the needs of the area. They begged ECM to consider coming in and lending a hand. So—we would not be stepping on the feet of other agencies. They would welcome us. One excuse down.

Next, I shared my burden with my husband, along with the invitation from Action International. To my surprise and delight, John readily agreed. He had also been feeling burdened for the helpless children of northern Uganda whose lives were being so totally destroyed. Another project would be challenging, but John felt that somehow, God would supply. Two excuses down.

Finally, I shared with the ECM Board. Although usually hesitant to get involved in anything new, they agreed unanimously, quickly, and without question. Every member felt that God was calling us to do what we could to help those children.

Immediately, I began planning my first trip to Uganda. I discovered that some of the children from the north had escaped and were living in a section of Kampala (the capital city, in the south) called Kamokya (say Kah-**moh**-tchuh.) I planned a visit to this slum area.

I also went to the north to see Action International's work and to visit one of the shelters in Gulu town where children from the countryside flocked at night to sleep smooshed together like sardines on the floor of any available building. There in the city, they were relatively safe from marauding soldiers of the LRA. In the morning they would walk miles back to their homes. That first trip was mainly to learn more about the situation, to see what was being done by others, and to look for some ideas about what ECM could do.

Bible Camp lessons at Kamwokya school

We connected with Jane Kansime, headmistress at Kamwokya School. For many years she welcomed ECM summer teams to teach in the school. The classes were huge and hundreds of children came to Christ.

One year, we had a scary event that could have turned tragic. Somehow with people coming and going, a very young child set off to make his own way home alone. On the way, he got lost and failed to arrive home.

Terror struck at my heart the moment I heard the news. So many dangers lay in his path! Immediately I set off in the direction he was said to have headed, asking everyone I saw along the way if they had seen him, and knocking at many doors. We did not find him, so on the advice of our Ugandan co-workers, we arranged for a radio announcement on the local station. The next day, someone found him wandering around a busy street market close to a mile away. He was unhurt and did not seem to realize what danger he had been in.

After that we instituted stricter controls about young children leaving the program! How we thanked God for keeping him safe and helping him to be found!

The heart of the initial work was in Gulu District which had been the hotbed of the Kony kidnappings. When I visited the first shelter there in 2006, Kony's devastation to the area was winding down (he had moved to a different location), and most of the shelters had already closed. The devastation he left behind will take generations to repair.

Quickly the government wanted to break up the infamous IDP (Internally Displaced Persons) camps. They encouraged and urged people to return to their "homes." The trouble was that there were virtually no homes to return to. Homes, small businesses and churches had been burned. Even village wells had been destroyed.

After making arrangements for a team to minister in the IDP camp, local officials refused us permission! They said anything we did to help the camps would only encourage the people to stay, and the government wanted them to leave. Only by God's grace were we finally permitted to minister there. This continued twice a year for several years, during Christmas break and during summer vacation. Meanwhile, the people in the camp very gradually found ways to start over in their home locations.

Our approach was to hold a three-day "Day Camp", with a Bible lesson in a local church (a thatch shelter), lunch cooked on the site, games, informal educational activities, a first aid clinic, personal interaction with the children, and distribution of a piece of clothing to each child. The camps were very well-received and I think a joy to all who participated in them. I designed lessons I hoped would bring some healing and comfort to children whose lives had been devastated by war.

A tiny part of the Tegot Atoo IDP camp in 2006. The people live in the little round huts. The style is typical of northern Uganda, but the IDP camp was intensely crowded in comparison to previous villages.

At the first camp, we took information on thirty children selected by local leaders and used this to find sponsors for each one. This enabled them to go back to school, and enabled ECM to begin a Saturday club to help them spiritually, emotionally, socially, and to a degree educationally. It was the beginning of our child sponsorship program. As those children were sponsored, others were added.

Children at the IDP camp lined up to receive food, and eating.

Children listen to ECM Bible teachers at the Day Camp.

At first the children looked and acted like walking zombies. They looked sad and expressionless at the same time. Ugandan staff explained to me that most had been forced to kill their parents. This was so widespread that basically the Acholi had lost an entire generation. When some of the children eventually escaped from the LRA, they had to go to their grandparents. Not only were the grandparents economically ill-prepared to provide for them, but now after suffering the loss of their own children, they were taking in those who had killed them. The emotional and social impact was beyond devastating. However, after ministering there several years, very gradually we began to see some small improvements, and many of the children did eventually come to faith in Christ.

Often the simplest acts of kindness were the things God used to open hearts. I remember one lady who brought her son to the camp suffering from persistent diarrhea. We did not have a specific medication to help him. Then I remember the easy-to-make oral rehydration formula I had learned to make in Congo. It required a few simple ingredients. We had the ingredients, but no plastic bags or containers in which to put them. So I just dumped out a box of crayons and put the ingredients in the box, explaining to her how to use them. When we had prayed for her son, she surprised us by saying, "OK, now I'm ready to be born again."

What? We hadn't as yet even shared the Gospel with her, but we learned that the local church had done so many times. When she saw our simple act of kindness, her heart was opened and she was ready to respond. She did indeed receive Jesus that day. Besides that, her son soon recovered from the diarrhea as well.

Clean, Safe Water

John had grown concerned about the absolute devastation Kony's war had wrought in the villages of northern Uganda. Virtually everything had been destroyed. Of greatest concern to him were the wells which supplied drinking water to the communities. That need motivated John in 2010 to take specialized training in third-world water technology.

Then, with the help of American teams and our faithful Ugandan staff, he was able to drill successful wells for three villages, bringing them a safe water supply. And while we might not think it convenient to wait in line with our water jugs at the village well each day, it was definitely closer and more convenient than any previous source of water they had had.

Ralph Gerold and the Ugandan helpers who brought clean water to one of the villages destroyed by Joseph Kony's LRA.

Today we are thrilled that R.N. Catherine Hayes has joined the project. By Ugandan law, she serves in a local hospital, but also serves the Tegot project, helping in so many ways.

In August, 2022, the ECM newsletter, 'Hope Is Rising', featured a story about one of the girls from the Gulu District Project. I was immediately captured by her bright smile, but it also brought tears to my eyes, because I remember the 'dead' look on the faces of the Gulu children when we started work there. I knew Jesus was a Great Healer not only of bodies, but of minds and hearts and emotions. Otherwise I would not have thought ECM could do anything there. Still, I had felt that it would likely take generations for society to return to anything anywhere near normal in the area. The girl featured in the newsletter had completed her education and was now a teacher herself, a vibrant Christian seeking to point her pupils to the Savior. To realize that this degree of healing had taken place in just sixteen years was just amazing to me. I just wept when I remembered that God had enabled me to be a small part of that healing.

8. Seeing Children Rejected because of Albinism, N Uganda (2007)

We had seen many children with albinism from the beginning of our Congo ministry, but we didn't realize all the special problems they faced. They were commonly called "albino" (pronounced all-**bean**-oh), but the term didn't seem to carry the offensive edge to it that it sometimes does in America. It seemed that people simply used it in a descriptive sense to refer to people who had the genetic condition that caused them to lack pigment in their skin, hair, and eyes, and thus to turn out pinkish-white, with light blonde hair and pink eyes.

We did notice that they were prone to develop skin sores, but we didn't realize that they were despised and rejected. We didn't know they were sometimes even hunted, since it was believed their body parts might make powerful magic, useful for getting good luck, passing an exam, finding love, or getting rich. We didn't realize other children sometimes told them they looked like pigs, or that the father usually left the family when an albino child was born.

We were riding with an American team in Uganda when one of the team members noticed a young albino boy along the roadside. He was walking with his arm up in the air to protect his eyes from the sun. For some reason, most albinos also experience serious vision problems. The team member said, "I wonder if my sunglasses could help that boy," and she asked us to stop. She got out and offered her sunglasses to the boy. When he put them on, his arm immediately went down to the natural position. Those ordinary sunglasses couldn't help sharpen his vision, but they obviously relieved the strain on his eyes and made his life immediately better by allowing him to use his arm in normal ways. We were all thankful our team could be of some small help to that boy.

The experience also got me to wondering if we could not do something more substantial to help albino children. We began collecting sunglasses, sunscreen, lip balm, and protective hats. We knew these items could be a practical help to them, and also help to create friendship with them and their families. I researched albinism and wrote some simple teaching materials. I struggled to know exactly how to explain it, because albinism is a genetically-inherited condition, yet already we were dealing with fathers who deserted their families because they couldn't believe that they may have passed on albinism, as well as charges that witchcraft or infidelity must be involved. I feared that much emphasis on the genetic aspect may make a bad situation even worse. In addition, most of the readers would be people having little if any scientific background or understanding. I needed to write it in popular, simple, and positive terms. I did my best.

We encouraged our staff to reach out to albino children and their families, and to create friendships with them in order to share the Gospel. We advertised our materials in some of the local-language newspapers of Uganda, and sent out our teachings by email.

I was a bit disappointed that the written materials were never widely used, but one staff member taught them at several local schools. One very heartening response we received was from a teacher. She said she had an albino child in her class. She had not understood his condition and had no idea "what to do with him." She thanked us for our teaching, which had helped her to help the child learn and to encourage greater acceptance amongst the other children, and had given a few simple and practical ideas for improving the child's chance of succeeding at his education.

Later, Wayne & Bonnie Hollyoak became ECM missionaries to Uganda. They experimented with creating sunscreen from local ingredients, produced it and sought government approval to sell it. What an immense blessing that was!

Many staff members took an interest in reaching albino children in Uganda, where they were in constant danger from practitioners of magical arts. When Sophie Akello visited her home district, Tororo, she saw many albino children, and learned of others being hidden away, never permitted to go outside of their own homes. She took the initiative to take pictures, do interviews, and write an extensive report. When I received it, I took it seriously, took it to the ECM Board, and they approved the extension of ECM work into Tororo District. ECM's Tororo Hope Center was born!

Today, the children's work in Uganda is based around Saturday clubs in several "Hope Centers" in various locations. In virtually all the Hope Centers, ministry to albinos is front and center. The children have been able to share their problems and experiences on several radio programs and at least one TV program. They benefit greatly from the Saturday club experience, where they interact with other children who accept them as equals and as friends. The children of normal pigmentation also benefit as they learn to accept those who look different from them and those who have physical limitations and challenges. Everyone benefits from the program.

9. Children living under persecution S Sudan (2006)

My heart is always drawn to the suffering child, the mistreated, misunderstood, forsaken, lonely.

Another suffering group of children I had read much about was the children of South Sudan. I knew the issues were complex, but much of the suffering stemmed from the facts that the South Sudanese were 1) black, and 2) largely Christian. The northern people were lighter skinned and predominantly Muslim. I also knew there were resources in the south that were coveted by the north, and that they were persecuted and had wars waged against them.

God opened doors for me to do ministry twice in Southern Sudan. The first time, in 2006, John and I made connections with an evangelical orphanage at Nimule, just over the border from Uganda. I was already in northern Uganda, so we drove north and into Sudan from there. We visited the orphanage and took them some supplies and Bibles.

Then in 2012, I did a week-long Sunday school training seminar at that same orphanage along with my Ugandan helper Sophie. I was already in Uganda in the Gulu area in the northern part of the country, so we just traveled up some challenging dirt roads to the crossing into Nimule. At that point, we could see into DR Congo to our left, as well as Southern Sudan straight ahead. All the evangelical churches of the town attended, as well as the orphanage workers.

It was just after South Sudan had gained its independence. Spirits were high. Border officials did not even place an entry stamp in my passport, but issued me an entry "permit." The process of getting in was not difficult, but it was long, as they proudly brought out the documents of their newfound independence and displayed them for me to admire.

In Uganda, one drives on the left side of the road like they do in the UK, but in South Sudan, they drive on the right side like we do in America. It's a bit of a tangle at the border with everyone crossing to the opposite side of the road all at once. Fortunately, the traffic was not heavy.

The seminar was well-received and teachers were enthusiastic. I was never able to follow up further on the work in South Sudan, but I trust that seeds were planted that were helpful to teachers there.

10. Seeing Beggar Children--Karimojong & The Karamoja Homeland, Uganda

One year, I was in Uganda and went into a Coffee Shop to take a break. I ordered something and sat in a comfortable chair in front of a big window facing the street. There was a table there, so I began to work on some reports.

A little girl out on the sidewalk caught my attention. I estimated her to be three or four years old. She was sitting in the hot sun on a very hot sidewalk with no protection except her panties. She appeared to be alone, and was crying. From time to time people would toss some coins into her skirt and move on. I thought she must be thirsty. I ordered a juice, took one of my bananas, and went out to her. As she gulped the juice down and devoured the banana, a group of people turned up objecting to my helping her. They were her owners, who had been watching her from the opposite street corner. They wanted her to cry because that brought more sympathy, and thus, more money.

Upon investigating, I found that nearly all the children begging on the streets of Kampala were members of a despised ethnic group called Karimojong. They came from Karamoja, in the northeastern part of Uganda. Many of those in Kampala had been trafficked here, while others came to the city looking for a better life.

Karamoja[xxxiv] is a cattle-raising tribe that lives a primitive life compared to their city cousins. They are experts in all things related to cattle, but know little about the modern world. They speak their own language, too, only distantly related to the Luganda spoken in the city. Arriving in the city, they have nothing, and often shelter together in group tents with dirt floors. Lacking sanitation, their habits and persons are not up to the standards expected in the city. I think it is no exaggeration that they are neither understood nor appreciated in Kampala. The contempt with which they are treated is hard to overstate.

As I learned more about the Karimojong, God laid on my heart a desire to help them and to bring Jesus to them. Most held on to their traditional worship of spirits.

The Project that was eventually designed for the Karimojong included visits to their enclaves to express a desire for friendship and the selection of some children to be sent to school through child sponsorship. Our staff found a private boarding school with caring Christian teachers that afforded some protection for the children and was close enough for parents or relatives to visit. We were assured that the children got enough to eat, improved hygienic conditions, and basic health care. On Sunday they walked to church together and found an accepting welcome by a local congregation.

These children started school knowing mostly only Ikarimojong. In school they had to interact in Luganda and learn English as well. What a surprise when we got their first report cards! The Karimojong did better than any of our other children. It appeared that they were really quite intelligent, acquired new languages easily, and were highly motivated to succeed.

In time many of them became Christians. Thank you, Jesus, for building your church amongst the Karimojong! One day, I was visiting the Kampala Karimojong and was asked to teach them. They all listened intently, but when I came up to the time to invite children who had not done so to trust in Christ as Savior, a girl, about twelve years old, sitting in the middle of the front row, fell to the floor and began jerking and crying out. I considered whether she might be having a seizure, but since the episode happened at the exact moment of the invitation, I also suspected demonic activity. I had seen similar things in the idol shrines of Ghana.

The girl was unconscious, so I asked my coworkers to carry her outside. I quickly finished the invitation and asked a helper to continue the teaching with the group. I went outside, where a coworker and I quietly called the demon to come out of her. Demons do not normally respond to my commands instantly as they did with Jesus, but I knew that as a believer I had authority over them, so I kept commanding them in His name to leave. In awhile the girl recovered. She had an amulet around her neck, and she agreed to give it to us to be destroyed, and we burned it on the spot. Thankfully, the other children did not seem at all frightened by the experience.

One year, I visited the mothers of the Karimojong community in Kampala. What whooping and shouting filled the street as they danced me down to a simple shack where they met regularly with ECM workers. To welcome me, they formed a circle and did a jumping song. Believe me, the Karimojong are strong jumpers! I couldn't measure, of course, but it seemed like they were jumping a yard into the air. A couple of feet at least, repeatedly.

The Homeland Project

As we became more familiar with their plot, we realized that the extreme poverty in the Karamoja Homeland was providing an inviting platform for child traffickers. As long as their children were starving, it would be easy for traffickers to convince parents that they might be able to give them a better life in the city. We began to think about a program to decrease the appeal of the traffickers by creating a sponsorship program in the Homeland.

I, Lorella, was never able to travel to the Homeland, but God did give me the privilege of developing the first broad outlines of the project, "selling" it to the ECM Board (easily), and helping to find some of the first sponsors for the children.

11. Seeing Children Taught by Teachers with no Lessons and no Bibles--The Mwinda Project, Congo, (2015)

By 2014, we were growing weary. No. we were not tired of what we were doing, but we were growing physically weary. In 1997, the Board had asked us to become International Directors. The current director, Floyd Bertsch, had inherited a home in Florida and decided to move there. I remember the Board saying to us, "You are the ones who have all the original stories." We were home at the time, and Congo was in turmoil as long-term president-dictator Mobutu was forced out of office. We weren't sure how soon or if we would be able to continue work in Congo. We had seen the board's offer as an opportunity to expand ECM's reach to African children in other countries, and at the same time to strengthen the organization so that work in Congo could hopefully continue in the future. In those years, 1997-2014, we saw ECM grow to have major centers, through the projects I have described, in Ghana (West Africa) and Uganda (East Africa), as well as Congo (Central Africa). I visited each of those countries at least once a year, sometimes twice, with John or with small teams. In addition, I was able to do Sunday school training in Togo, Benin, Uganda and South Sudan, and to speak at a conference in Nigeria.

Sidenote: At one of those trainings in Uganda, I noticed our driver, Kibuule, talking to the pastor during the break. I had been teaching about how to lead a child to Christ. Soon he came to me and announced, "Mama, today I took Jesus as my Savior." Glory, Halleluya! Kibuule was a Muslim and spoke only a little English. We had hired him as our driver for many years, and he had served us faithfully. Each team that had come out to Uganda had prayed for him and done their best to witness to him both by life and by word. At last that Gospel seed that so many had watered with their prayers sprang to life. Kibuule continues to drive ECM teams today, and is still trusting in Jesus.

Back to my story--As directors, we traveled most weekends representing ECM at churches and mission conferences and Sunday school conventions. I particularly loved teaching workshops at the Urbana Student Missions Conferences, Sunday School Conventions, STEER, etc.. However, as time went on we realized we were getting very tired, and it wasn't the kind of tired that a rest or a vacation would help. As we aged, we were gradually slowing down, and the travel in particular was wearing us out.

After prayer and consideration, we decided to step down from our leadership position as International Directors and go back to "just" (haha) being missionaries with ECM. This meant we would no longer receive support from ECM's general budget, as we had while we served as International Directors. We agreed to raise our personal support for the second time, since our personal support had, at our request, been absorbed into ECM's general budget while we were directors. We agreed to seek mostly new partners so that the ECM general budget could remain as strong as possible.

Mark Luckey, one of ECM's missionaries to Uganda was chosen as the new director. He asked us to focus our energies on Congo, and that felt like a natural choice for us as well.

As I prayed about this change in our lives, recognizing increasing challenges in mobility as my osteoarthritis got worse and worse, I asked the Lord, "What can I do now that will make the biggest contribution at this stage of my life?" Almost as soon as I began praying, it was clear to me what the answer was.

I had invested much effort in training teachers and 'teachers of teachers' to reach children for Christ. My idea for many years had been to teach the Congolese how to find a narrative of an event directly in the Bible and develop a lesson from it.

As time went on, I realized that it was one thing to recite "the four main parts of a lesson." It was an entirely different thing to develop a lesson directly from the Bible with no guide whatsoever. It was an even bigger thing to continue doing that week by week.

I began to notice a disturbing pattern. Whenever I visited a Congolese Sunday school, which I did at every opportunity, I would find that I could almost predict what lesson would be taught. It could be one of three choices—either Jesus welcomed the children, or John 3:16, or, perhaps 80% of the time, 'children, obey your parents'.

While all of these are good lessons, I began to realize what was happening. The Bible was a big, largely unfamiliar book, and carving a lesson out of it was hard work. VERY hard, for many of them. In their frustration, I found most teachers reverting to familiar, easy subjects. I was forced to admit that perhaps we need teaching guides that will carve out a bit of Bible truth and help teachers frame it into a lesson for children. I recognized that in my teaching and in my writing and in my linguistic experiences, God had uniquely prepared and qualified me for just such a task.

As I continued praying, He laid on my heart the vision of writing a set of teaching guides that would bring children through the main events of the entire Bible. I envisioned a ten-year time frame, since a Congolese child from a Christian family is commonly in Sunday school from about the age of 5 until he is about 15.

How would the lessons reach the churches? We could sell them, but there are very few Christian bookstores in Congo, and transport to get to them is very expensive. The large churches in the city might be able to afford the books, but they would be out of reach of the many smaller village churches. I decided to try distributing them through small distribution centers scattered throughout the country. I called them "Teachers' Resource Libraries." Churches could borrow the materials, then return them to constantly get new resources. I believed this plan would get the needed help to the largest number of churches possible.

To print such Sunday school lessons in the quantities needed and to transport them to the "Teachers' Resource Libraries" for distribution would be costly. ECM could not afford such an expense from its general budget, I knew. I volunteered to try to raise the substantial budget for this project. To distinguish it from our personal support and from other ECM projects, we chose the name, "The Mwinda Project." 'Mwinda' means 'light' in Kikongo and several other Congo languages. With the Sunday school lesson guides, we were seeking to bring the light of God's Word to the new generation in Congo.

As I write this book, lesson guides for much of the Old Testament have been completed. Since the lessons follow Bible history from Creation on, I chose to write them in chronological order. (That is largely, but not completely the same as Biblical order. We group Bible books by the kind of writing—history, poetry, prophecy. The poetic and prophetic books fit into the historical framework.)

It has been quite a challenge. I want to put in as much 'meat' as possible, but the constant cry I hear from teachers is to keep it short and simple. Their reading level is not the same as mine, for the most part.

Many teachers have difficulty distinguishing instructions to them and teaching for students. For example, if I write, "Teacher, ask the children to clap their hands," instead of stopping and asking the children to clap their hands, many will simply read, "Teacher, ask the children to clap their hands," and go on as if those words were part of the Bible story.

My mind has been filled constantly with questions about what events should be included in the lessons and which must be left for a later time, since the number of events greatly exceeds the number of weeks available for teaching them. It's an exciting project, and the adventure continues!

Music for Teaching

Another aspect of the Sunday school lessons is the music that accompanies the lesson. Congolese churches love music, and most of it has some teaching value. However, I encourage the teachers to sing or teach at least one song that reinforces the specific teaching of the day. When I look at the songs most commonly sung in Congo, I find lots of amazing praise songs, but far fewer songs that reinforce the teaching points I need. So along the way, I have collected, translated, and written many songs for use in Sunday school. When I was living in Africa, I was actively teaching these songs, but now that I am no longer there, and with the Sunday schools now multiplying at such a rapid rate, I find that many teachers look at the words and want to sing them with their kids, but have absolutely no idea how to do so.

So, in the past few years, I have been trying to develop the idea that we could find musicians to play the songs and record them. Gradually we have built up a small team that includes home schoolers, a pastor's entire family with a range of ages, and Carolyn Smith, our pastor's wife, who is a skilled musician. Regulars are my friend Margie Jackson who has a low voice like mine but less scratchy and much richer, and Jim Sawatsky a retired missionary who had a music ministry in Congo.

Out of the 156 songs I have assembled for the Sunday school songbook, we have recorded 50, and many of these we have visualized and put up on YouTube to give access to as many teachers and children as possible.[xxxv] We are trying to find inexpensive flash drives that are compatible with cell phones in Congo to help us distribute the songs to all our trainers.

Kids' Radio

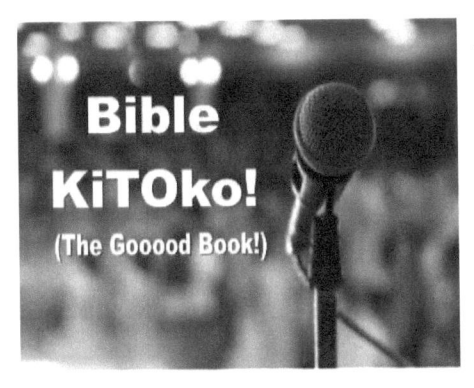

Bible KiTOko! (The Gooood Book!)

A third part of the Mwinda Project is my kid's radio program in the Kikongo (Kituba) language. "Bible Kitoko!" roughly means what we mean when we say "The Good Book." I am privileged to be able to present this program on "Radio Nkembo" from the Nkara mission station where our family worked our first term in Congo. I don't use my name with the radio program. I simply refer to myself as "Mama Ecodime"—Mama Sunday School. However, the first time the program was broadcast in Congo, some people recognized my voice and called in to the station asking if I was back in Congo and was there at Nkara. Yes, it is amazing even to me that I can sit at my computer here and record programs that reach people throughout almost all the Kikongo-speaking region of Congo.

For a kids' radio program I use a voice much different from my everyday conversational voice. I find that when I exaggerate emotions to the max as I am recording, when I play it back it doesn't sound exaggerated at all. It sounds just right.

So, when I first began recording, I was using my very-excited radio voice, and our dog Lola thought I was in trouble. She is so protective! She came racing in to my rescue, then came to a quick stop and sat there looking around, obviously confused. Where were my attackers? In time, Lola did get used to my radio voice.

12. Seeing the Deaf (Congo, 2022)

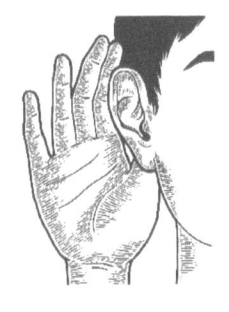

For the past few years, I've had increasing mobility issues due to severe osteoarthritis throughout my entire body. I'm still getting back to Congo once a year, although the trip is increasingly painful. I also speak on occasion at the supporting churches for the Mwinda Project, but otherwise I try to stay put as much as possible, enjoying the quiet of our own home and the opportunity to use my computer as a weapon in the war for the Kingdom of God. I thought my days of developing and promoting new projects were over.

Then one day this last summer (2022), John had gone to bed early and I flipping through TV channels to find something to watch while I worked on visualizing Bible verses for the Mwinda Project. I noticed a show on TBN called "Finishing the Task." It talked about people groups that were still counted as unreached as far as the Gospel is concerned, having no Bible, no church, and no access to a believer or a group seeking to bring the Gospel to them. They were seeking to mobilize the body of Christ to pray over these groups and to find churches or missions to "engage" them. The subject of reaching the unreached has long gripped my heart, so I got on my computer and called up their website, finishingthetask.com. I clicked on the list of remaining people groups and was astounded to find that it began with a list of deaf people groups. Several of them were in Africa, and one right next door to ECM work. The unreached deaf of Congo-Brazzaville were listed at 13,000.

I began a web search to find out all I could about deaf ministry, the Gospel needs of the deaf, and what was being done to reach the deaf in Congo. From the beginning, it was as if God was holding my hand, leading me on step by step. For over a week, I could hardly stop or do anything else. I realized that God still had one more group to which He wanted to open my eyes.

I learned that worldwide, the deaf are amongst the least-evangelized groups of people. In developing countries, there are few opportunities for deaf people and little understanding of the issue. Parents are often unable to communicate with a child born deaf, and written language is also difficult, based as it is on sounds.[xxxvi] In Africa, children born with any kind of disability or any unusual traits are often believed to be cursed. Sometimes it is assumed that they are born as a result of marital unfaithfulness. Parents are confused, ashamed, and afraid. Many of them hide such children in a dark room of the house, and some abandon them.

Because it is difficult for a child born deaf to talk, it is often assumed they must also be unintelligent. In reality, the deaf have the whole range of intelligence just as the hearing do, but without communication, it is difficult for parents to recognize this. Whether in the family, in school, in the church or in the society at large, communication with the deaf is difficult or impossible without sign language. Therefore, deaf people are often profoundly alone and unevangelized. This problem is exacerbated in places like Africa where "healthy-wealthy" teaching is so common in the churches. If God wants everyone to be healthy, how are we to understand His intention for the deaf?

As I understood more about the situation of the deaf, I realized that God had not brought this to my attention so that I could just store away the information. He was asking me to do something about it. I knew I couldn't go to minister to them myself, but I could research the issue and call ECM's attention to it. I work closely with the national leadership in Congo, so I could draw their attention to it and help them design a project to begin reaching the deaf. I could use my writing skills to help interest others in helping. So I persisted.

I learned that there were several active deaf ministries in DR Congo, but all to the east. Since a huge rain forest and an utter lack of navigable roads separates eastern Congo from central and western Congo, that was far, far away for all practicable purposes.

One of the inspiring and encouraging things I learned concerned an African-American man named Andrew Foster. He had started the first deaf ministries in eastern Congo. Foster became deaf at age eleven as a result of two severe illnesses that followed one upon another. He loved to learn, and was able to attend a school for black deaf children in his home state in the southern U.S. when segregation of the races was still standard. That school only went through the sixth grade. Upon completion, Foster was told that black deaf boys could go no further.

Andrew Foster (Photo from Wikipedia Commons)

He heard of a school for black deaf children in Michigan, where his aunt lived. It was an effort to get all the way to Michigan, but he endured, led on by the vision of continuing his education. In Michigan, he found he was a few months' short of being 18, the minimum age for the school. He could wait a few months, but then he also learned that he was ineligible anyway, because his parents did not reside in Michigan. What if they moved into the state? No, they needed to live there a longer time.

His hopes of attending high school dashed, Foster began working. Eventually he completed high school through correspondence. Next, he applied to Gallaudet University, a college for deaf students in Washington, D.C. They had never admitted a black student. He was turned down. He tried again, but his application was again rejected. He tried a third time, and was once more turned down.

A counselor advised Foster that he might have a better chance if he completed more education first, any kind of education. So, he attended a business college in Detroit, while still working a full-time job. He learned skills like bookkeeping and typing. Then he applied for the fourth time to Gallaudet and was accepted—with a full scholarship! He was their first black student.

Eventually the boy who was told he could not go past sixth grade earned two Master's degrees.[xxxvii]

During his years with his aunt, he had become an earnest, committed Christian. He had also met a missionary from Jamaica who had spoken at a Sunday school class, and had felt God's call to become a missionary himself. So upon completion of his second Master's degree (one in special education and one in Christian ministry), he moved to Ghana, West Africa. There, he started the first school for the deaf in Africa, outside of Egypt and South Africa. He found families who were hiding their deaf children and a government that did not believe the deaf could learn.

Using a combination of every method available, he was successful in educating the deaf. After spending several years in Ghana developing his methods, he went on to establish 22 deaf schools[xxxviii] in 13 African countries. Most of them also had attached churches for the deaf. Sadly, he died in 1987 in a small plane crash while going from eastern Congo to Kenya to visit his schools.[xxxix]

As I learned all I could through the internet, I also asked our Congolese staff to investigate the situation on the ground there. Our Congo Director, Pastor Mupepe, was able to locate five

Pastor Mupepe (ECM Congo Director—wearing the tie) with leaders of one of the deaf communities in Kinshasa

deaf communities[xl] in Kinshasa. The leaders of one of the largest groups told him that they were started in 1979 by an African-American missionary named Andrew Foster. Bang-zoom! Foster had named a pastor to help them, but that pastor had since passed away, and the spiritual state of the group had diminished greatly. The other four groups had never been evangelized.

Pastor Mupepe and I worked together by email to develop a substantial report along with recommendations for beginning ministry, which we presented to ECM's International Director, Mark Luckey. He was excited by our report, feeling it fit in well with his own vision for ministry. He accepted our suggestions for a beginning budget for deaf ministry to be included in ECM's 2023 budget.

As I look back, I realize that again and again, God used my painful childhood to prepare me to see the hurting, the neglected, the isolated and marginalized. Did He give me autism? Maybe. If He didn't cause it, did He allow it? Maybe. Either way, it was His gift. It was His gift to open my eyes to see lonely, hurting children who needed His love. Because He gave me eyes to see and a heart to feel the pain of the downtrodden, I have been privileged to be a part of blessing many lives. Thank You, Jesus! The little pain I felt is nothing compared to the joy of bringing the Good News to Africa' hurting children. Thank You, Jesus, for doing whatever You needed to do, to give me eyes to see.

Epilogue

As I have written this book, I have been reminded again that even with God's help, there is no way John and I did all this alone. So very, very many people have contributed along the way. The list of names at the end of the book doesn't even begin to scratch the surface. Besides the weekly volunteers mentioned, countless others helped with banquets, garage sales and other events, websites, translations, fundraising, giving, prayer, encouragement, counsel, and much, much more. Also, the Americans mentioned as short-term missionaries served alongside African partners in most cases. I apologize that there is no way I can include them all. I am encouraged to know that "God is not unrighteous to forget your work and labor of love" (Hebrews 6:10). Thank you and may all you have given boomerang back to you in blessings abundant.

Lorella Rouster

210

TIMELINE

1980-God calls John to serve as a missionary in Africa as John is milking his cows.

1981-1984 Rouster family serves in Zaire (now DR Congo) with AMG International at Mission Nkara, First village Sunday schools started in area around Nkara. Cindy Hawkins lives with Rousters for 9 months, teaching John Henry.

1985-Every Child Ministries (ECM) is founded with the help of Christian friends.

1985-1990-Rouster kids finish high school in U.S., Lorella develops teacher training program for Sunday school, Summer teams to Zaire train teachers and expand Sunday schools.

1988-While doing a teacher training center at Lako Mbulu, Lorella is shown an ideal location for a training center.

1989-Lorella takes intensive French studies in Quebec, John, Lorella & Kristi travel to Zaire to inspect the location for a training center, local chiefs agree to give ECM the land. Floyd Bertsch named International Director.

1990-John Henry Rouster (our son) graduates from high school, John, Lorella, John Henry, and Kristi move to Zaire to start a new mission for a Training Center.

1991-1998-Rousters develop "Mission Garizim" as a Training Center for "Teachers of Teachers".

1992-Erik and Bambi Carlson serve with Rousters at Mission Garizim. Erik helps build an airstrip and Bambi works with the women.

1997-Zaire is renamed 'The Democratic Republic of Congo.' Laurent Kabila seeks to take over Congo from dictator Joseph Mobutu. Kabila's soldiers 'visit' Mission Garizim.

1997-Rousters become International Co-Directors.

1998-War in Congo forces the Rousters to return to the U.S., Sunday schools hit the 1,000 mark, Grant enables ECM to print 10,000 copies of Sunday school training manual in Kituba, Lingala, Tshiluba, and French. (40,000 total)

1999-With Congo closed to outsiders at the time, ECM sends its first team to Ghana, W. Africa. John, Lorella, and Allan Cox conduct Sunday school seminars and explore ministry needs. School ministry begins in Ghana. It never "took off" in Ghana as it had in Congo, but another organization still continues occasional training of teachers using my materials.[xli]

1999-"Teaching for Africa" website begins to make training materials available online to African churches. Still functioning today.

2000-Ministry begun to shrine slaves in Ghana, continues until 2016.

2000-Ministry to street children begins in Ghana, continues until about 2014.

2002--Street ministry leads to the establishment of Haven of Hope Home for Children in Ghana.

2004—January 22-Shrine slaves freed from Aklidokpo Shrine in Ghana

2004--Haven of Hope Academy opens in Ghana.

2005, December 9--Shrine slaves freed from Sovigbenor Shrine in Ghana

2006—ECM begins ministry in Uganda with emphasis on war-affected children. Child sponsorship begins to support that ministry. ECM directs its ministries to the Tegot Atoo IDP (Internally Displaced Persons) camp.

2006—First visit to South Sudan, Orphanage

2006—Lorella speaks at church conference in Nigeria

2008--ECM begins ministry to Karimojong street children in Kampala, many of whom were trafficked.

2010—The Way Home Project with Russ and Marcia Baugh becomes associated with ECM in Uganda

2010—John takes Third-World Water technology training with Equip, International

2011, 2013—John drills wells in Uganda Gulu District with American team

2011—Mark & Stacy Luckey and family join ECM with the Afayo Project

2012--ECM begins ministry in the Karamoja homeland of Uganda in an effort to prevent child trafficking at its source.

2015--Rousters relinquish International Directorship, become ECM missionaries once again. Mark Luckey is named International Director.

2016--Lorella begins devoting her attention again to Congo and starts the Mwinda Project to provide Sunday school literature in local languages.

2017--John officially resigns from ECM due to health issues. Lorella continues as missionary with John helping on a volunteer basis.

2019--Lorella begins "Bible Kitoko", kids' radio program in the Kituba language

2020-- Lorella begins recording and visualizing Sunday school songs to help teachers learn and teach them more effectively. She is later joined by retired missionary Jim Sawatsky, Margie Jackson, and a team of local volunteers.

2021-- Sunday schools in Congo pass the 5,000 mark. Lorella begins mentoring Pastor Mupepe who is installed as Congo Director following Pastor Mayele.

2022-- Lorella is on target to complete Sunday school lessons through the Old Testament by the end of the year.

2022-- Lorella starts an ECM Congo YouTube channel & puts up the Sunday school song videos.

2022-- Lorella becomes aware of the deaf as an unreached people group. With Congo staff, she researches the problem and organizes a plan to reach the deaf of DR Congo and Congo Brazzaville.

2023-- ECM scheduled to begin ministry to deaf children and families in Kinshasa.

ENDNOTES

[i] John and I had previously made a short visit to Zaire in January, 1981, to better understand what we were getting into and to help us know how to prepare for life there. The whole family arrived in June, 1981.

[ii] The first Sunday school was started at Mission Nkara Ewa where we and the Smith family were living, on September 13, 1981. We had been there not quite three months.

[iii] Now Nicol Sponberg

[iv] Records show that in reality, 57 attended that first Sunday, 107 the second Sunday, and 300 the third. Many were from surrounding villages. After that attendance settled down to around 80, although it was lower during school breaks.

[v] The people were then called Zaireans, the country Zaire. It became Congo when Kabila took power after Mobutu. I use the words Congo and Congolese for consistency throughout the book, since I'm referring to the same country and people.

[vi] Nkara village in January, Longo and Nsiengobo in February, Mpene, Mibiere and Niadi in March, etc.

[vii] Our family was able to live during those years on John's salary plus income from the sale of our farm. We began receiving support from ECM only when we returned to Zaire as missionaries in June 1990.

[viii] Kituba (also called State Kikongo), Lingala, Tshiluba, French, Portuguese, and finally, English.

[ix] See chart of Short-Term missionaries following these endnotes.

[x] Besides our three biological children, we had adopted a Congolese daughter, Kristi, in 1982 while we were living at Nkara Ewa.

[xi] At that time, the Bandundu Province included the Kituba-speaking area south of the Kasai River, and the Lingala-speaking area north of the Kasai. The southern part is largely savannah (grasslands), while the northern part is almost entirely rain forest, with a very large lake, the Mai-Ndombe. In 2015, the country was reorganized into much smaller units, and what had been the Bandundu Province became three provinces—Mai-Ndombe to the north, Kwilu and Kwango to the south. Our work was based in what is now Kwilu Province.

[xii] Kristi came to us in October, 1982 from the medical clinic John was overseeing. She had severe bronchitis and was weakened from malnutrition following her mother's death. The nurse said Kristi needed some extra TLC if she was to have any chance of living, so we took her into our home temporarily. She gradually gained strength. Since her family had not been able to care for her in the village, they agreed to allow us to adopt her. Kristi was eventually adopted three times—by tribal agreement, by Zairean law, and by American law. She remained with our family wherever we went and was eventually naturalized as an American citizen.

[xiii] Congolese have frequently told me that the one good thing the Belgians did for them during their colonial rule was to introduce French. It is not that French is a better language than Congolese languages. They just realized that they needed a national language to unify the country and to facilitate commerce, education, and travel. Yet if anyone had tried to make one of the Congolese the national language, it would likely have resulted in fighting, many groups vying to see their own language be chosen. Further, if anyone in power had imposed his own language on the country, it would have been changed immediately as soon as the next person took power. An outside language was able to unify them and provide long-term stability.

[xiv] Kristi's birth name was Kikula Somo. When we adopted her, we made her first two names her middle name and gave her the first

name Kristianne. So her full name became Kristianne Kikula Somo Rouster. She was commonly called "Kiki", and later "Kristi."

[xv] We kept in touch with annual Christmas cards. Many years later one of the cross-Africa adventurers began long-distance biking riding with his wife. Biking from the east coast to the west, they stopped by at our country home for lunch, then biked to the ECM office where they took pictures in front of the sign there before venturing on their way.

[xvi] Other "critter" stories were shared in my first book, "God Uses Crooked Sticks".

[xvii] Chuck later served many years as a board member and Chairman of the Board.

[xviii] Kinshasa's population is now over 17 million (2021 estimate).

[xix] Congo-Brazzaville comes into play again in ECM's ministry to the deaf. See Chapter 12.

[xx] After being ousted by Kabila's forces, Mobutu fled to Morocco, ending his 32-year autocratic rule. He died there in 1997, and Congo refused to allow repatriation of his body to his home village. That's an enormous insult in African culture.

[xxi] ECM was officially incorporated in Ghana that same year, 2000.

[xxii] The capital city of Ghana

[xxiii] See the list of short-term missionaries and helpers at the end of this book.

[xxiv] Demands of staff on the shrine slavery project forced us to choose between projects. In order to raise their wages, we had to close both the school and the street ministry projects. I often regretted that decision, and even moreso after the slavery project was closed.

[xxv] "Sadam" came from a Muslim family. When he was about to enter his teens, his grandfather showed up and took him from Haven of Hope. To my knowledge, the boy had never professed faith in Christ, but we know he heard the Gospel over and over. We pray that the seed planted may yet sprout and find good ground in his heart.

[xxvi] Unfortunately, we eventually had to drop the Congo Street Ministry because we found that one of the leaders had been turning in false or exagerrated reports. I know that it began well, and I am still not sure where it went wrong. When we realized the worker had been untruthful in reporting, we gave him the opportunity to correct it, but he resigned instead.

[xxvii] See the list of short & long term missionaries at the end of the book, listed by year.

[xxviii] Officially speaking, an orphanage receives only children whose parents have died. A children's home receives children from difficult backgrounds for whom the normal family situation was not working for one reason or another. Haven of Hope receives both. We received some children whom Ghana's Social Welfare Department had taken from dangerous family situations.

[xxix] There was never any compromise of principle. Compromises were made on the procedure and parameters of the partnership. IN had experience and ECM, at that point, was the new-comer and the learner in the partnership.

[xxx] The group at times denies the existence of the practice, at other times acknowledges it, but says the women in it are treated like queens. Whether they acknowledge the word or not, they approve the practices of which we are speaking.

[xxxi] Idols usually belong, not to an individual, but to a family, and are passed down in the family line.

[xxxii] This was extremely rare, but shrine slaves and devotees ran a whole spectrum, and how they became attached to the shrine was one item on the spectrum.

[xxxiii] This event preceded our calling to the Karimojong children of Uganda. I included that event under 'Fighting Child Trafficking at the Source' in order to put like things together. I felt this would be easier to follow than a straight timeline of events, which would have mixed together the development of all the various projects. For more clarity timewise, consult the timeline at the end of the book.

[xxxiv] Karamoja is the land. Karimojong are the people. Ikarimojong is their language.

[xxxv] Our YouTube channel is called 'Ecodim Congo'.

[xxxvi] Written language is much more readily developed by those who were born hearing but became deaf later in life, because the concept of sound is already established.

[xxxvii] Later on, he also was awarded an honorary doctorate from Gallaudet, the school that had earlier rejected him three times. Thus, in later life he was referred to as "Dr. Foster."

[xxxviii] Foster established more deaf schools and churches than anyone else anywhere.

[xxxix] There were no survivors of the crash. Foster, along with the other victims, is buried in Rwanda at the site of the accident.

[xl] Not all communities are geographically-based. The deaf, for example, tend to be drawn to one another by common problems, interests, and experiences.

[xli] "Heroes Under God" led by Thompson Afari uses my training materials by permission.

Short-Term Missionaries & Others Who Shared Our Journey (1983-2015): (A few have been ommitted for security reasons.)
John led most of the building teams, while I led most of the School Ministry and Shrine Ministry teams.

Zaire/Congo

1983-84 Cindy Hawkins

1987 Jack Krajnak, Sharon Rouster

1988 Carrie Rouster

1989 Kristi Rouster

1990 John Henry Rouster

1991 Floyd and Hildred Bertsch, Chuck Daily, Kristin Lund, Vanessa Slosson, Ron Smith

Bill and Carrie Boehmer

1992-1993
Erik and Bambi Carlson-11 months

1995 Hilary Welborne, winner of the Children's Bible Contest through AWANA Clubs, with mother, Carey Kinsolving, and videographer

David Bryant, Tami Lape, Kristen Maurer

1996 Floyd Bertsch, Stephanie Kiefer

2007
Kurt Jarvis, Sharon Corcoran Jerry Storz, and Donna Ytes of the International Network of Children's Ministries Training Team, with Dr. Dale Garside of Evangelism Resources as translator

Ghana
1999 Allan Cox

2001
Esther Ntoto and a student team from Vanguard University: Chelsea Belardo, Marissa Emde, and Elizabeth Sedmak.

School Ministry--Ron Corrigan, Michelle Gerold, Abigail Kean, Barbara Wiles, Wendie Willis, Carla Yerga, Amanda Zuidervart

2002
School Ministry-Haven of Hope--Leslie Bailey, Lana Foster, Andy Munson, Nicole Sobol, Barbara Wiles

2003
School Ministry, Haven of Hope--Leslie Bailey, Valerie Betts, Michelle Gerold, Felicia Luke, Linda McCollough
Pastoral Training-- Elder Talmadge Betts, David Bryant, Pastor James Ford

2004 Shrine Slavery
Jenny Reid, Ed White of Great Commission Resources

2004 School Ministry
Leslie Bailey, Valerie Betts, Jordan Bixler, Cheryl Cramer, Stephanie Franco, Lindsay Kimball, Kathy Mark, Jessica Mathison, Lois Pope, Marie Thomas

2004 Pastoral Training Ministry
Elder Talmadge Betts, Pastor James Ford

2005
Laura Gillaspy-Haven of Hope Academy, 1 year

Pastoral Training Ministry-
Pastor James Ford, Elder Talmadge Betts, Sampson Green

School Ministry--
Stephanie Bailey, Cheryl Bockstahler, Alyson Murtiff, Claudia Parker, Ben Pitzen, Emma Semtner, Katie Suitor

Al & Kitty Rickert-Vision Tour
Frank and Stacia Hall
Dustin Marr
Presley & Kelly Reader
Kristen Hall

John Henry Rouster-Haven of Hope, solar

Sunday School Training--Kurt Jarvis, Weldon Lemke, Training Team from International Network of Children's Ministries

2006 School Ministry
Ruth Alexander, Cheryl Bockstahler, Leanne Kauffman, Rachel Key, Elaine Martinez, Debe Paul, Rae Lynn Rawlins, Joel Rogina, Whitney Rouster, Dorothy Uhrhammer

2007
Veronica Rollins-Vision Tour

School Ministry & Haven of Hope- Cheryl Bockstahler, Kassie Dantzler, Ron Dillon, Ashley Ducommun, Stacy Hoenig, Travis Plympton, Gloria Shin

Rebekah Branaman, Lisa Mims

2008
School Ministry & Haven of Hope- Miranda Benefield, Jennifer Blocher, Cheryl Bockstahler, Natalie Crawley, Elveria Ferguson, Crystal Hieb, Cory Rice, Sarah Rice, Katie Swisher, Lucretia Tolliver

Ashleigh Ducommun Reiss-Haven of Hope-1 year

Haven of Hope Activity Center-Tom Harmon, John Jones, Dave Riley, Joe Roberts

2009
Lindsay Hendrix-Haven of Hope Academy, 1 year
Elise Messner-Haven of Hope Academy, 1 year
Lana Foster-Haven of Hope

Micky Beaujean-Ministry to former shrine slaves

Jim & Carolyn Driscoll—Career, still serving

2010

Shrine Slavery Project--Sharon Aldrich

School Ministry & Haven of Hope-
Holly Bowers, Hannah Howard Dillon, Ashley Ducommun, Caitlyn Enyeart, Mirae Nace, Rachel Spencer

2010-2011
Laren Botts, Haven of Hope Academy, 1 year

2010-2011
Amanda Smith, Haven of Hope Academy, 1 year

2011-Haven of Hope, Haven of Hope Academy Team—Cheryl Bockstahler, Nathan Edwards, Tammy Ng, Nathan & Lindsay Palmer

2012
James & Denese Forkkio-Long Term
Doug & Sally Wayner-Haven of Hope, Long Term
Slave Project Building Team-- John Jones, Dave Randolph
Slave Project Vocational- Sharon Aldrich

Haven of Hope, Slave Project--Marissa Boehmer, Whitney Rouster

Haven of Hope- Cheryl Bockstahler, David Bryant, Donna Cunningham, Jenny Emmanuel, Josh & Jordan Gesimondo, Janice Higgins, Dayton Lavender, Monica Miles, Amanda Smith

Karen Harkness-Haven of Hope-Long Term

2013

Tiffany & Roxanne Easter
Shrine slavery project, vocational-Sue Daily, Nancy Gushee, Rebecca Koonce, Ruth Torrenga

Myron & Amanda Pincomb, Shelly Keels and the Girls for Africa Team-Haven of Hope Academy

Shrine slavery project, vocational-Sharon Aldrich

Whitney Rouster

Haven of Hope-John Henry Rouster

Haven of Hope, AIDS Hospice Care-Hannah Howard Dillon

Haven of Hope-
Jim & Carolyn Driscoll-Career, still serving in Ghana
Jere & Ruthann Gowin-Long Term

2014
Shelly Keels-Haven of Hope

Uganda
2006 Restoring Children of War, IDP Camp Ministry-
Sharon Aldrich, Hazel Hermosillo

2007 Restoring Children of War, IDP Camp Ministry-
Lance Bernhard, Heather Hernandez, Stacy Hoenig, Amanda Kedzierski, Leanne McKitirck, Gloria Shin, Megan Towell

2008 Restoring Children of War, IDP Camp Ministry-
Matt & Brecka Arnett-One year
Nancy Cardoza-Long Term
Christine Sliwinski-Long Term

Renee Banke, Lee Carnahan, Jodie Donahue, Hannah Gibson, Kendra Lyman, Marjorie Nelch, Sean Parsons Katie Rousseau, Deborah Tsuschida, Becca & Luke Voight

2009
Nancy Cardoza --Long term
Sarah Dingus (5 months)

Catherine Hayes-Career, Still serving
Rebecca Davis, Jamie Dischoff, Jodi Donahue, Adam Johns, Brooke Jones, Hannah Gibson, Debi Howey, Megan Lange, Kendra Lyman, Marjorie Nelch, Kitty Rickert, Melissa Rogers, Katie Suitor Luke & Becca Voight

2010
Ashley Bentz-6 months
Angela Gast—1 year
Tawnee Martin-1 year

Cheryl Bockstahler, Caitlin Enyeart, Brooke Jones, Ellie Morse, Debe Paul, Bethany Strand

Deaf Education--Jennifer VanderMolen

2011 Water & Medical Education Team
Bobbie Buck, Ron Corrigan, Kelly Cupell, Don and Barbara Davis, Angela Ghast, Dave Riley, Glenn Scott

2011 Preventing & Fighting Human Trafficking Team
Wendy Bartel, Brenda Huffstetler

2011 Restoring Children of War Team
Brooke Dresser, Megan Dunklin, Adam & Stacy Johns, McKenzie Hyde, Kelsey Leonard, Jaimie Lipton

2012-2013 New Year's with the Karimojong
Sue Daily, Katie O'Farrell, Linda Power, Ronda Slawinski

2013 Afayo Project-Courtney Wrinkle

2014 Chris & Michelle Fisher & family-Long Term
Bruce & Janine Coker & family-Afayo Project-Long Term
Ralph Gerold-Water Team

2015 Margie Jackson

Togo & Benin
2009 Sunday school training--Hazel Hermosillo, Lois Pope

Board Members 1985-2014

Trish Allee, Rosemary Archbold, Leslie Bailey, David Bryant, Allan Cox, Becky Crum, Chuck Daily, Judy Ericson, Bonnie Faurote, Linda Haddix, Tommy Johnson, Joseph Joniec, Onika Khomo, Jack and Susan Krajnak, Carl and Lee Lane, George Maddox, Kurt and Kim Minko, Jerome and Joane Nelson, Myron Pincomb, Robert Pressler, Richard Ready, Vernon Robinson, Wally and Ella Wyman

Home Staff and Major Volunteers

Sharyl Albright, Roberta Alexander, Gertrude Anderson, Dick and Med Bashore, Carol Baunuch, Gordon Becker, Hildred Bertsch, Helen Bollen, Bob Brown, Anita Buibish, Allan and Faye Cox, Denise Elder, Sandi Enyeart, Bonnie Faurote, Danette Figueroa, Karen Fleming, Mike and Carol Froege, Ralph and Ruth Gerold, Nancy Gushee, Sherry Hamby, Lew and Pat Horner, Jo Howerton, Roni Hoyle, Margie Jackson, Ginger Kassie, Mary Keller, Tom and Holly Keithley, Helen Kron, Tami Mahns, Al McLendon, Monica Miles, Ruth Nelson, Dick and Pat Norris, John Henry Rouster, Jim Sawatsky, Agnes Schoon, Rachel Shields and The Shields family, Katie Suitor, Rhonda Tomich, Tammy Vogel and the Vogel family, Wally and Ella Wyman

Many others generously gave of their time and effort in special events, home projects, web design and more, including of course prayer, encouragement, and generous giving. Thank you to each one who has so selflessly served! We appreciate you all.

One of my greatest fears in publishing a list like this is that I may leave someone out. My sincere apologies if I have neglected to mention anyone. We appreciate every contribution. Contact me concerning any mistakes or ommissions and I will gladly correct them in future editions.

Other Books by Lorella Rouster:

God Uses Crooked Sticks—Our Family's 30+ years' Adventure of Learning & Growing in Africa (2017)

Stoke My Fire-- Favorite Missionary Stories, 2022

More Books in the Making! Stay in touch to hear about the latest.

Lrouster@ecmafrica.org

Subscribe to my free monthly newsletter, "Rousters' Real Deal" to keep up-to-date with the Mwinda Project and the unfolding ministry to the deaf. (Request at e-mail above.)

Or sign up at https://www.mwindaproject-ecm.com